recipes for parties

To my parents Jim and Marie—the ultimate party people.
—*Michael Leva*

For my aunt Gay, with much love.
—*Nancy Parker*

menus, flowers, decor:
everything for perfect entertaining

recipes for parties

michael leva & nancy parker / photography by pieter estersohn

RIZZOLI
NEW YORK

New York · Paris · London · Milan

CONTENTS

**Foreword
by Serena Bass**

When Michael Leva invited me for dinner to his house in Connecticut, I had no idea what was in store. Having been the event planner at some of the most extravagant celebrity weddings and New York City galas, I will admit to feeling a bit jaded concerning parties. On the whole, the ambience, the presentation of the food, the actual food, and the environment created . . . I thought I had seen it all.

So I have to say it was truly thrilling to find so many unexpected, clever ideas and whimsical touches conjured up by Michael and Nancy Parker, his coconspirator at the Connecticut dinner, and in this book. As the evening progressed, I also recognized the solid, practical behind-the-scenes planning, which would inevitably make any party flow and succeed.

The brilliance of that particular gathering, plus the ten festive occasions in *Recipes for Parties*, are captured—and, more importantly, clearly explained. It is indeed a fascinating and useful book. It appears Michael and Nancy have coined a new phrase, "practical creativity," and the results are tangible on every page. Make it beautiful and make it work, is evidently their mantra.

These days, it is not enough to offer an entertaining coffee-table tome with pretty, impossible-to-emulate images. In order to justify buying a volume such as this book, you need the authors to work generously on your behalf and offer considerably more. I have often looked for an entertaining guide that could successfully encompass the disparate realms of inspiring photographs (the flowers, the food, the linens, the lighting), motivating recipes that actually turn out brilliantly, and a practical countdown to help you pull everything together. And now, miraculously, here it is.

You will discover inside not only those invaluable things already mentioned but also insight into making and sending invitations, how to create the ambience you are aiming for, and choosing what kind of music and when to play it. The biggest plus are the tips and "cheats" at the beginning of every chapter, which when followed, will make your next foray into entertaining a decidedly happy occasion for both you and your guests. What more could one want from just one book?

Introduction

Entertaining can often seem daunting. After all, who has the time, energy, and know-how to throw a really good soiree? It is a common misconception that only those proficient at pulling off parties should entertain. And yet this should not be the case.

Becoming thirty was a turning point from going out all the time to staying at home surrounded by friends. But moving away from nights on the tiles that ended at 4 a.m., smoky-eyed and bleary, there was a part of me that squeaked in fear, "Am I heading down the path of stuffy dinner parties?"— the kind I could not imagine ever throwing. I used to be terrified that an evening of entertaining at home would involve catching glimpses of my guests while dashing between the kitchen and dining room, carrying dishes of overdone or underdone food, or having to endure watching my dearest friends give each other sympathetic glances. Why would people risk throwing a dinner party that could be a possible disaster? These were my feelings on the matter before meeting Michael several years ago in New York City on a business trip when we happened upon our mutual love of entertaining. From then on our transatlantic friendship bloomed. Whenever we were on the same continent, Michael and I happily hosted joint parties for our friends in Connecticut, New York, London, or the British countryside. Together we discovered the long-forgotten art of how to entertain and enjoy oneself in the process.

Michael's love of cooking and creating memorable parties stems from his mother, Marie Leva, a talented home cook. Marie has never called in the caterers. If she invites a hundred guests for cocktails at her home in Florida, she makes every hors d'oeuvre herself. Her lessons on cooking and entertaining have been invaluable to Michael. I was introduced to entertaining from an early age. My grandmother was obsessed with hosting regular cocktail parties. I loved to observe her bygone party etiquette. And having a successful food photographer, Gina Harris, for a mother provided me with an in-depth understanding of food styling. As a child I spent many hours in the photographic studio watching ad campaigns for Cadburys, Schweppes, and cookbooks come together.

The beauty of throwing a bash is that it can be whatever you want it to be. Since you create the atmosphere, you are not at the mercy of anyone else's rules. There is a sense of cozy exclusivity entertaining at home surrounded by your handpicked crowd—whether it is a simple supper with six best friends or a large outdoor cocktail party. To my surprise, I have attended far too many dinner parties where the host and hostess look utterly relieved when the guests trickle out of the door. Yet that awkward feeling is not necessary. Our book functions as a guide to easy, yet impressive, entertaining and includes steps to help throw stress-free parties that both you and your guests will remember.

Our Recipes for Success

First and foremost, create a guest list with due care and attention. Consider which friends will mingle well. I have a group of girls that I consider my "facilitators." I can drop them into any social situation on their own and they work magic. When selecting reliable friends to help a party run smoothly, often they are not the loudest or craziest of your peers but instead the ones with the most social poise. Do not be afraid to have a broad range of guests, including lone rangers. Singletons make an event go with a bang, as they always have the best stories tucked up their sleeves.

One of the essential tools of being a host or hostess is etiquette—the basic guidelines boil down to courteous manners and a touch of common sense. As guests arrive, they are coming into your domain, and the first and most important thing to do is to make them feel welcome. Greeting them should be done in a relaxed manner—whether it is the Southern European cheek-kissing ritual, the more formal British handshake, or the American hello and hug. Do not forget to introduce them to friends they may not already know. If guests arrive with flowers, thank them graciously and explain that you will arrange them later (place the flowers in a bucket or a sink full of water). Settling guests is the most important task at hand.

With greetings and introductions made, now is the time to serve drinks. Should guests offer to help out, give them a task, as this is an ideal ice-breaker. Do not rush guests into the dining room; instead allow them the chance to meander and get to know each other. When dinner is ready, usher them to the table. Part of the preparty planning should include forethought on the seating arrangement.

Setting a special tone for your party is vital. Thought should be given to food presentation, decor, and, of course, yourself. You want the first guest who walks in to realize that you've paid attention to creating a special mood. Whenever possible, Michael loves to light a fire before guests arrive. He also has accumulated a cache of flatware and glassware in beautiful colors and shapes to be able to create striking tabletop combinations. A mix of high-end accessories, such as antique creamware and vintage Venetian glasses, with the low—lab beakers for flowers and simple cotton napkins— is his ideal.

Having a well-stocked pantry and bar are crucial for easy entertaining. Our list of food essentials includes a variety of salts (fleur de sel, kosher, coarse, flaked, and fine sea salts), peppers (black and white peppercorns, peperoncino (red pepper flakes), cayenne pepper), oils (good-quality extra virgin olive oil and canola oil), and vinegars (aged balsamic vinegar and aged sherry vinegar). We also recommend having a good Dijon mustard (preferably Grey Poupon) and several cans of San Marzano whole plum tomatoes, as well as such spices as allspice, whole nutmeg, cinnamon sticks, and star anise on hand. Basic baking ingredients include all-purpose flour, baking powder, yeast, superfine sugar, and honey. Regarding fresh ingredients, make purchases the day of and the day before the party. We try to use fresh herbs and seasonal produce, as food that has not traveled halfway across the world in a crate tastes a million times better. As for the bar—it should be stocked with a variety of liquors, including vodka (We prefer Grey Goose, Stolichnaya, and Absolut.), a good-quality gin (preferably Tanqueray or Bombay Sapphire), Campari, vermouth, Cointreau, brandy, and bourbon, as well as angostura bitters and simple syrup (either prepared or homemade; see recipe on page 94).

Each chapter of this book breaks down how to achieve a look for a variety of occasions through the use of color, flower arrangements, beautiful table settings, and flattering lighting. Remember, planning ahead and allowing plenty of time is the key to being a calm and successful host. Finally, feel free to cut corners by following our list of "cheats" provided for each party. The aim is to have fun, and if that involves supplementing your cooking by bringing in prepared food, hiring a bartender, or bribing friends' children to serve and tidy up, then so be it. I always bear in mind the wise words of my grandmother—"Darling, nobody wants to be served by a limp hostess."

moroccan buffet

COCKTAILS
Pomegranate Sour Mix
Souk Sour

HORS D'OEUVRE
Citrus-Marinated Olives

MAIN DISHES
Mechoui (Roast Leg of Lamb
   with Cumin and Salt)
Baked Black Sea Bass with
   Tomatoes, Onions, and Olives
Yam Salad with Golden Raisins
   and Toasted Pine Nuts

Tomato Salad with Preserved
   Lemons and Chive Blossoms
Spiced Couscous
Carrot Salad with Chiles
   and Cumin
Fennel and Radish Salad
   with Oregano

DESSERT
Cardamom Ice Cream

SERVES 10

LEFT: A taste of Marrakech—our languorous guests dining while the sun sets.

Late June ushered in the beginning of a glorious summer, which we celebrated with a Moroccan buffet held on a New York City roof terrace overlooking a private park. The event was a re-creation of a thirtieth birthday party I had thrown for my husband, Buck, in Marrakech for our New York friends who had been unable to attend. Michael and I chose this North African-inspired buffet, as this cuisine allows you to prepare the dishes well in advance. We wanted the entire evening to be about relaxed and intimate dining. The ambience was established by seating our guests at low tables on throw cushions and rugs. We managed to bring a hint of the souk to the city.

THE LOOK

For the Marrakech theme, we set out low tables for dining and jewel-toned throw cushions, and laid some North African ikats on the floor. A hot and sultry night dictated casual, summer clothes—simple cotton dresses, shorts, and wide-legged trousers.

THE MOOD

Music
It is important to play music that evokes your chosen theme. In this case we selected music with a North African vibe set to an accelerated pop beat.

Lighting
We created hurricane lamps by taking large straight-sided glass vases and filling them a quarter full with sand. Ivory church candles were placed in the sand. The tables were dotted with small glass votive candles.

Flowers
Pink gerbera daisies have a summery feel and are a simple adornment. We placed several of them in aluminum pots. Clay planters can work just as well if sprayed silver. Soak a block of oasis (floral foam) until saturated in a bucket of water. Line each pot with aluminum foil (if there is a drainage hole), and fill with oasis that has been cut to fit snugly inside. Using a chopstick, poke holes in the oasis to allow easy insertion of the daisy stems. Start arranging the flowers from the center. Working in a spiral pattern, overlap the petals of the flowers so there are no bare spots.

Invitation
This event was planned last minute, so a flurry of phone calls and e-mails sufficed as invitations.

THE PLAN

The day before

/ Compile to-do lists.
/ Check the weather report. If inclement weather is in the forecast, be prepared to set up the party inside.
/ Go to your speciality food store and fish and farmers' markets to buy the buffet ingredients.
/ Make the Cardamom Ice Cream.
/ Marinate the olives in the citrus and herbs.
/ Prepare the *chermoula* rub for the Baked Black Sea Bass with Tomatoes, Onions, and Olives and the *mechoui* rub for the *Mechoui*.
/ Slice yams for the Yam Salad with Golden Raisins and Toasted Pine Nuts; store in plastic bags and refrigerate.
/ Clean and prep the carrots for the Carrot Salad with Chiles and Cumin.
/ Prepare all salad dressings.

The morning of

/ Arrange the tables and set out cushions and rugs.
/ Place the handmade hurricane lamps and fill with sand and candles.
/ Compose the flower arrangements.
/ Rub the lamb with *mechoui* spices for the *Mechoui*.
/ Coat the black sea bass with the *chermoula* for the Baked Black Sea Bass with Tomatoes, Onions, and Olives.
/ Make the Pomegranate Sour Mix.
/ Parboil the carrots for the Carrot Salad with Chiles and Cumin.
/ Toast the pine nuts for the Yam Salad with Golden Raisins and Toasted Pine Nuts.

Last minute

/ Bake the leg of lamb in the oven for 4 hours before serving. Baste regularly.
/ When guests arrive, put the fish in the oven for the Baked Black Sea Bass with Tomatoes, Onions, and Olives.
/ Boil the yams for the Yam Salad with Golden Raisins and Toasted Pine Nuts.
/ Assemble all salads and dress them.
/ Prepare the Spiced Couscous.
/ Make the cocktails.
/ Assemble the platters attractively, and set out on the buffet table.

CHEATS

A buffet is itself a cheat because the food is laid out informally for the guests to serve themselves. We presented the buffet under a canvas pergola to protect the food from the sun and heat. An ordinary garden umbrella would work just as well. Traditional Moroccan cooks prefer preparing couscous by taking the many hours necessary to steam the grain to perfection. However, we feel that instant couscous is just as good and foolproof. The salads are also cheats, as they too can be prepared in advance. We have included a recipe for preserved lemons, but it is labor intensive. Instead, you can buy preserved lemons from a specialty food shop. The Cardamom Ice Cream recipe is well worth the effort and can be made ahead of time. Alternatively, there are excellent artisanal ice creams that you can purchase.

moroccan buffet

COCKTAILS

Pomegranate Sour Mix

This exotic mixer can be added to soda water or lemonade for a nonalcoholic version to the Souk Sour (recipe follows).

{ Makes 3 cups, or enough mix for at least 6 cocktails }
1/2 cup fresh lime juice
1/2 cup fresh lemon juice
1/2 cup pomegranate juice
1/2 cup Simple Syrup (see recipe on page 94)

Combine all the ingredients in a pitcher and stir. Refrigerate until ready to serve.

Souk Sour

For guests with a sweet tooth, dampen the rim of a highball glass with water and dip in sugar prior to filling with ice and Souk Sour.

{ For each cocktail }
2 ounces vodka
3 ounces Pomegranate Sour Mix (see recipe above)
3 or 4 pomegranate seeds and a sprig of mint, for garnish

Pour the vodka and sour mix into a shaker full of ice and shake vigorously. Pour into a highball glass filled with ice. Serve with a few pomegranate seeds and a sprig of mint.

HORS D'OEUVRE

Citrus-Marinated Olives

Adding your own touch to store-brought olives gives them extra flavor. You can store covered in the refrigerator for up to three weeks.

{ Makes 3 cups }
1/2 Preserved Lemon (see recipe on page 19)
3 cups cured green and black kalamata olives
1/2 teaspoon peperoncino
1/2 teaspoon ground cumin
3 tablespoons finely chopped Italian parsley
2 garlic cloves, finely chopped
3 tablespoons fresh lemon juice
1/3 cup extra virgin olive oil

Rinse the preserved lemon with tap water and pat dry. Remove the pulp and membrane and finely chop the rind. Place the olives, chopped rind, and all the other ingredients in a serving bowl and mix well. Cover and refrigerate until ready to serve. This dish can be made a day ahead.

LEFT: Our exotic Moroccan buffet set out to enjoy.

18   moroccan buffet

Preserved Lemons

These lemons take six weeks of preserving before they are ready. It is well worth the wait, as they can be kept indefinitely. You can also purchase preserved lemons at a speciality food store.

{ *Makes 1 1/2 quarts* }
1 1/2-quart preserving jar, which has been sterilized
2 cups coarse sea salt
3 star anise
5 whole cloves
18 firm lemons, scrubbed and dried
1 cinnamon stick
2 bay leaves

Layer 1 inch of salt on the bottom of the preserving jar. Add the star anise and 2 of the cloves. Cut off the top and bottom of each lemon. Slice vertically from the top to 1/2 inch from the center. Flip the lemon over and repeat. The lemon should be almost cut in half, held together by an inch of flesh. Turn the lemon on its side and cut to 1/2 inch from the center. Repeat on the opposite side, cutting almost to the center. The lemon has now been almost quartered, leaving an inch of flesh holding the fruit together. Pack the vertically quartered lemon with as much salt as possible, making sure not to tear the lemon open. Push the lemon down into the bottom of the jar. Repeat this process with 14 of the lemons.

Once the lemons have been squeezed into the jar, evenly distribute the remaining 3 cloves and star anise. Push the cinnamon stick and bay leaves into the jar. Juice the remaining 3 lemons and pour over the cut and salted lemons in the jar. The juice should cover the top lemon by 1/2 inch. If there is not enough liquid, top with tap water. Seal the jar and leave at room temperature for at least 6 weeks prior to using.

MAIN DISHES

Mechoui **(Roast Leg of Lamb with Cumin and Salt)**

Mechoui, a traditional Moroccan lamb dish, bakes at a low temperature for a long time but needs to be basted often. It is delicious served at room temperature, making it the perfect meat for a buffet.

{ *Serves 10* }
5 tablespoons unsalted butter, softened
2 tablespoons ground cumin
2 teaspoons coarse sea salt
1 tablespoon ground coriander
One 5-pound leg of lamb, butterflied, rolled, and tied

Preheat the oven to 350°F.

In a medium bowl, mix the butter with the cumin, 1/2 teaspoon of the salt, and the coriander to form a paste. Coat the lamb with the butter mixture, making sure the paste covers all the folds of the rolled meat. Place the lamb on a rack in a roasting pan and bake for 2 1/2 hours, basting every 20 minutes with the juices from the pan, until the meat has a crisp crust and the inside is pink and tender. Remove the lamb from the oven. Let the meat rest for 20 minutes, then cut into thick slices, arrange on a serving platter, and serve. Mix the remaining cumin and salt in a small bowl and use for dipping.

LEFT: *Mechoui* on a bed of grape leaves.

moroccan buffet

Baked Black Sea Bass with Tomatoes, Onions, and Olives

Chermoula, a traditional Moroccan marinade, guarantees a moist and succulent fish. With a relatively short cooking time, the sea bass can be slipped into the oven at the last minute.

{ Serves 10 }
2 whole black sea bass, 2 1/2 to 3 pounds each
1/2 cup chermoula
2 1/2 pounds ripe plum tomatoes, thinly sliced
Fine sea salt
2 cups green kalamata olives, pitted and sliced

Preheat the oven to 425°F.

Wash and pat the fish dry, and rub inside and out with *chermoula*. Cover with plastic wrap and marinate for 2 hours in the refrigerator.

Place the fish on a baking dish and lay the tomato slices on top, overlapping the slices 1/4 inch in a scalelike pattern. Sprinkle with salt. Place in the oven and bake for 35 minutes, or until cooked through and tender. Remove from the oven, transfer to a serving platter, and scatter the edge of the dish with olives. We recommend placing half an olive over the eye. Serve immediately.

Yam Salad with Golden Raisins and Toasted Pine Nuts

Served hot or room temperature, this dish is ideal for a buffet as you do not have to worry if it has completely cooled down.

{ Serves 10 }
4 yams (about 2 pounds), peeled and sliced into 1/2-inch-thick pieces
1 cup golden raisins
1 medium onion, thinly sliced
1 teaspoon paprika
A pinch of sea salt
1/2 teaspoon plus 1 pinch peperoncino
2 tablespoons extra virgin olive oil
1/2 cup toasted pine nuts

Put the yams, golden raisins, onion, paprika, and a pinch of both salt and peperoncino in a medium saucepan. Add 1 1/2 cups water, cover, and bring to a boil over a medium-high heat. Boil for 5 minutes, then reduce the heat to medium-low and cook for another 5 to 7 minutes, until the yams are tender. Pour out any liquid that has not evaporated.

Transfer to a serving bowl and drizzle with the oil. Sprinkle with the 1/2 teaspoon peperoncino and the pine nuts and serve.

PREVIOUS SPREAD: *From left to right, clockwise:* Having a great time from dusk until twilight at our Moroccan feast. Laid out for guests: simple white plates, some with fanciful scalloped edges, which are paired with crisp white linen napkins and silverware. RIGHT: Yam Salad with Golden Raisins and Toasted Pine Nuts in an old ironstone bowl.

23

Tomato Salad with Preserved Lemons and Chive Blossoms

Use heirloom tomatoes when possible, as the range of colors makes this dish a visual delight, especially when combined with delicate white or lilac chive blossoms, which have a slightly milder flavor than the stalks.

{Serves 10}
6 heirloom tomatoes
2 Preserved Lemons (see recipe on page 19)
1 red onion, finely chopped
1/4 cup extra virgin olive oil
4 teaspoons fresh lemon juice
1/2 teaspoon paprika
Fine sea salt
Freshly ground black pepper
1 bunch chives, with blossoms

Slice the tomatoes as thinly as possible and arrange on a platter. Cut the preserved lemons into quarters and remove the pulp and membrane and discard. Rinse the rind, pat dry, and cut into fine strips. Distribute the onion and lemon rind evenly over the tomatoes.

In a small bowl, whisk together the oil, lemon juice, and paprika. Season with salt and pepper. Pour the dressing over the tomato slices. Cut the chives into small pieces with scissors and scatter over the salad. Place a few blossoms on top and serve.

Spiced Couscous

We always make an extra amount of this dish as it makes great leftovers. Use cold as the bottom section of a layered salad.

{Serves 10}
4 cups organic low-sodium chicken stock
2/3 cup currants
3/4 teaspoon fine sea salt
1/4 teaspoon ground allspice
2 cups instant couscous

In a medium saucepan, combine the stock, currants, salt, and allspice. Place over medium-high heat and bring to a boil. Add the couscous and boil for 2 minutes, stirring constantly. Remove from the heat, cover, and let stand for 5 minutes. Fluff with a fork and serve.

LEFT: Three temptingly fresh salads: fennel, tomato, and yam salads.

**Carrot Salad
with Chiles
and Cumin**

Carrots, a traditional side dish in Morocco, combine perfectly with this spicy dressing.

{ Serves 10}
2 pounds sliced lengthwise baby carrots
3 whole garlic cloves, peeled
1 teaspoon fine sea salt
1/3 cup extra virgin olive oil
1 1/2 tablespoons white wine vinegar
1/2 teaspoon peperoncino
1 1/2 teaspoons paprika
1 1/2 teaspoons ground cumin
1 bunch Italian parsley, finely chopped
1 bunch cilantro, finely chopped

Put the carrot slices and garlic in a saucepan and cover with water. Bring to a boil over medium-high heat, then cover and boil for 4 minutes, or until the carrots are al dente. Plunge into an ice bath to set the color and stop the cooking. Discard the garlic cloves. Drain and dry the carrots, sprinkle with salt, and place in a serving bowl.

Whisk together the remaining ingredients in a small bowl. Pour the dressing over the carrots and serve at room temperature.

**Fennel and
Radish Salad
with Oregano**

This pretty salad is a refreshing accompaniment to the spicy dishes on our menu.

{ Serves 10}
4 large fennel bulbs
1 bunch radishes, thinly sliced
1 cup fresh oregano leaves
1 cup extra virgin olive oil
Coarse sea salt

Trim the bottom and stalk off each fennel bulb and set aside. Cut out the root end of each bulb. Slice the bulbs as thinly as possible from root end to tip. Arrange the fennel slices on a platter. Top with the radishes and oregano. Drizzle with the oil, season with salt, and serve.

RIGHT: Carrot Salad with Chiles and Cumin in a French creamware platter with a curious serpentine serving spoon.

moroccan buffet

DESSERT

Cardamom Ice Cream

Letting the crushed cardamom pods steep slowly in the heavy cream gives this exotic ice cream its subtle flavor. We like to serve this dessert with fresh figs and a drizzle of lavender honey.

{ Makes about 1 quart }
8 whole green cardamom pods, lightly crushed
2 cups whole milk
1 1/2 cups heavy cream
1 vanilla bean, split lengthwise
4 egg yolks
3/4 cup sugar

Pound the cardamom pods with a mortar and pestle and place them in a cheesecloth bag. Put the milk, heavy cream, vanilla bean, and the cheesecloth bag of cardamom pods in a saucepan and bring just to a simmer over low heat. Turn off the heat, cover, and let rest for 20 minutes to allow the flavors to infuse. Remove the vanilla bean and scrape the vanilla seeds into the cream mixture. Remove the cardamom pods.

In a mixer, cream the egg yolks with the sugar for approximately 4 minutes, or until a pale ribbon forms. Beat a ladleful of the warm cream mixture into the egg yolk-sugar mixture. This will temper the eggs so they do not curdle. Then pour the entire egg mixture into the saucepan and whisk thoroughly. Return to low heat and continue to whisk until the custard is thick enough to coat the back of a spoon. Remove the pan from the heat and cool, then refrigerate until cold, at least 2 hours. Freeze in an ice-cream maker following the manufacturer's instructions.

THE OUTCOME

The heat of the June day was entirely evocative of Marrakech while the eastern flavors were the perfect counterpoint to the western setting. Buck was thrilled to have two birthdays, the second so reminiscent of the first that our dear friends in Manhattan felt as if they had joined the Marrakech Express. Far below we could see the streets teeming with weekend revelers as we settled back onto throw cushions in our lofty retreat. Michael and I were rewarded for our culinary efforts as we watched guests gorge themselves on our fragrant lamb and fish, happily licking lips and fingers. Laughter broke the warm night air as tales were recounted against the hum and buzz of our New York backdrop.

RIGHT: Gray glazed bowls set off Cardamom Ice Cream with fresh figs.

a simple supper

SERVES 6

LEFT: Lighting the chandelier candles sets an intimate mood for dinner.

A simple supper is a lovely and easy way to entertain. A small gathering of close friends for a quiet dinner allows for intimate conversation. This dining experience can be pulled off with a minimal amount of effort without losing its elegant touch. For our supper, held in Michael's candle-lit Connecticut dining room during the fall, we gathered together a carefully chosen circle of friends. We prepared hearty dishes amenable to advance preparation, so we had the luxury to relax and enjoy each other's company. Everyone relished our little feast in such visually stunning surroundings.

THE LOOK

Surrounded by one's closest friends in the comfort of home, there is the temptation to dress casually. Though we do not advocate formality for such an occasion, a pretty silk dress for girls and smart cashmere sweaters for boys is appropriate. Against the backdrop of Michael's dining room, with its Merchant and Ivory overtones, we used antique creamware along with individual Wedgwood pots for the Favorite Chicken and Mushroom Pie. Splashes of color—red and fuchsia floral arrangements—enlivened the neutral canvas.

THE MOOD

Music   Be careful to keep the music low so as not to overpower the conversation. We love jazz, so Michael softly played an upbeat jazz mix that he had put together for a party mood.

Flowers   We arranged single blooms fresh from the cutting garden—red zinnias, giant castor beans, amaranth, and dahlias—in chemistry vials. These very simple floral arrangements are an inexpensive way to add a whimsical touch.

Invitation   An invitation is not necessary to an informal event such as a simple supper. A phone call or e-mail at the last minute is just fine.

RIGHT: Angels and Devils on Horseback and cool Real Gin Martinis compete for our guests' attention.

THE PLAN

The
day before

/ Compile to-do lists.
/ Shop for all ingredients.
/ Prepare pastry for the Favorite Chicken and Mushroom Pie and refrigerate.
/ Make the Almond Cookies.
/ Prepare the blackberry syrup for Fall Berry Fool.

The
morning of

/ Prepare Angels and Devils on Horseback. Cover in plastic wrap and refrigerate.
/ Lay out serving pieces and glassware, and set the table.
/ Arrange the flowers.
/ Make the Favorite Chicken and Mushroom Pie but do not bake.
/ Make the Fall Berry Fool and chill.
/ Mix up the French Dressing for the Perfect Green Salad.

Last
minute

/ Prepare the Perfect Green Salad.
/ Bake the Angels and Devils on Horseback.
/ Make up the Real Gin Martinis.
/ Put the Favorite Chicken and Mushroom Pie in the oven.

CHEATS

If you're pressed for time or not feeling energenic, the most obvious cheat is to buy ready-made pastry for the Favorite Chicken and Mushroom Pie. Bakery cookies may be substituted for the Almond Cookies. If purchasing cookies, make sure they have a subtle flavor that will not overpower the Fall Berry Fool.

COCKTAIL

Real Gin
Martinis

Since a Real Gin Martini is about the marriage of subtle flavors, it is vital to use a good-quality gin and dry vermouth.

{ *For each cocktail* }
1 1/2 ounces Bombay Sapphire gin
1/2 ounce Noilly Prat dry vermouth
1 green olive or lemon twist, for garnish

Fill an iced metal cocktail shaker with gin and vermouth. Shake for 30 seconds and pour into a martini glass. Garnish with an olive or lemon twist.

HORS D'OEUVRE

Angels and Devils on Horseback

I cannot remember who introduced me to the delights of Angels and Devils. This hors d'oeuvre is so simple to prepare and so divine that I have made it countless times.

{ Serves 6 }
6 slices bacon
10 pitted dates
10 sage leaves
1 tablespoon extra virgin olive oil
2 sprigs dill, separated into leaves
10 sea scallops

Preheat the oven to 400°F. Grease a baking sheet and set aside.

Cut each bacon slice into 1 1/2-inch-wide strips. You should have a total of 20 strips. Wrap each date with a bacon strip. Dip the sage leaves into the oil to prevent them from burning, and wrap a leaf over each bacon-covered date and set aside. Wrap a dill leaf over each scallop, then cover with a bacon strip.

Lay out the bacon-covered dates and scallops on the prepared baking sheet. Place in the oven and bake for 15 minutes, or until the bacon is cooked and the bacon fat has crisped. Remove from the oven and cool to room temperature before serving.

MAIN DISHES

Shortcrust Pastry

This is a basic shortcrust recipe that can easily be scaled up, following a ratio of two parts fat to one part flour. Substituting the salt with 2 tablespoons superfine sugar makes a sweet version that is perfect for tarts and flans.

{ Makes enough pastry to top 6 Favorite Chicken and Mushroom Pies }
3 cups all-purpose flour, plus 1/2 cup for dusting
1 teaspoon fine sea salt
1/2 cup lard
1/2 cup (1 stick) unsalted butter, chilled and cut into pieces
4 tablespoons ice-cold water

In a large bowl, sift together 3 cups of the flour and the salt. Gently rub the lard into the flour. Cut the butter into the flour and lard mixture and rub together, aerating with a tossing motion so as to keep the lard cool and prevent the butter from melting. Once the mixture has the texture of lumpy sand, add the water, 1 tablespoon at a time, until a doughlike consistency forms. Cover in plastic wrap and refrigerate for 30 minutes.

Remove from the refrigerator and bring to room temperature, then roll out on a floured work surface as directed in the Favorite Chicken and Mushroom Pie recipe on page 36.

We especially like to make this pie the day after roasting a chicken, as any leftover meat and gravy can be used for this dish. All that is left to do is sauté the mushrooms and make a pastry topping. I have included my recipe for Shortcust Pastry. However, store-bought puff pastry is an excellent alternative, especially if you like its buttery flakiness.

{ *Serves 6* }
8 tablespoons (1 stick) unsalted butter
4 medium white onions, coarsely chopped
3 leeks, cut into 1/2-inch-long strips
1 1/2 pounds cremini mushrooms
3 pounds boneless, skinless chicken breast
1/4 cup plus 3 tablespoons all-purpose flour
3 1/2 cups low-sodium chicken broth
1 tablespoon Dijon mustard (preferably Grey Poupon)
1 cup dry white wine
2 teaspoons flaked sea salt
1 teaspoon freshly ground black pepper
1/4 cup finely chopped fresh tarragon
Shortcrust Pastry (see recipe on page 35)
1 large egg, beaten

Preheat the oven to 400°F.

In a heavy-bottomed pan, melt 4 tablespoons of the butter over medium heat. Add the onions and sauté until softened and beginning to brown, about 10 minutes. Add the leeks, reduce the heat to low, and cook for 5 minutes, stirring occasionally. Remove from the heat and set the leeks and onions aside in a bowl.

In the same pan, melt 2 tablespoons of the remaining butter over medium heat. Add the mushrooms and sauté until browned, about 10 minutes. Leaving the juice in the pan, transfer the mushrooms to the bowl of onions and leeks.

Roughly chop the chicken breasts into 1-inch cubes. Heat the remaining 2 tablespoons butter along with the liquid from the pan. Once bubbling, add half of the cubed chicken and cook until browned on all sides, about 5 minutes. Transfer the cooked chicken to a bowl, brown the remaining chicken, and transfer to the bowl. Sprinkle the cooked chicken with 3 tablespoons of the flour and stir to coat thoroughly.

Return the chicken to the pan and cover with the stock, mustard, and white wine. Bring to a boil, then immediately reduce the heat to low and cook, stirring, until the sauce begins to thicken, about 4 minutes. Add the reserved vegetables, the salt and pepper, and stir to combine. Add the tarragon and transfer the chicken mixture either to individual pie dishes or a large casserole dish.

To make the pastry lid or lids (depending on whether you are using individual dishes or a large casserole dish), lightly flour a work surface and roll out the pastry. Cut the pastry into a circular shape, making sure that it is a little bigger than the dishes selected. Dampen the edge of the dishes with water. Carefully cover the casserole dish or individual pie dishes with the pastry lid or lids, pressing the pastry down over the rim to create a seal. Cut the leftover pieces of pastry into a few leaf shapes to use to decorate the pies and arrange them on top of the pastry lids. Brush the top of the pies with the beaten egg.

Place in the oven and bake for 30 minutes, or until the pastry is golden and the filling is bubbling.

RIGHT: Piping hot Favorite Chicken and Mushroom Pie.

The Perfect Green Salad with French Dressing

The clean flavors of a green salad work perfectly alongside the richness of our Favorite Chicken and Mushroom Pie (see recipe on page 36), but it can also be served as a separate course.

{ Serves 6 }
2 heads Boston lettuce
3 bunches lamb's lettuce (mâche)
2 fennel bulbs, cored and thinly sliced
French Dressing (recipe follows)

Separate the lettuce leaves, discarding the outer leaves and the stalks. Wash the leaves thoroughly and gently dry in a salad spinner. Place in a large bowl with the fennel. Just before serving, toss the salad with the dressing.

French Dressing

{ Makes about 1/2 cup }
5 tablespoons extra virgin olive oil
3 tablespoons sherry vinegar
1 teaspoon Dijon mustard (preferably Grey Poupon)
1 teaspoon superfine sugar
1/2 teaspoon kosher salt
1/2 teaspoon coarsely ground black pepper

Place all the ingredients in a thoroughly clean glass jar. Screw on the lid and shake to combine. Refrigerate until ready to use.

DESSERTS

Almond Cookies

There is enough dough to bake an ample quantity of these addictive cookies. If you don't devour these sweets at one sitting, they store very well.

{ Makes 30 cookies }
2 1/4 sticks unsalted butter, softened
3/4 cup superfine sugar
1 large egg yolk
2 teaspoons almond extract
1 1/2 cups all-purpose flour
1/2 cup finely chopped blanched almonds

Preheat the oven to 300°F.

Using an electric mixer, cream the butter with the sugar until fluffy. Add the egg yolk and almond extract and beat until blended. Sift in the flour and beat at low speed to combine.

Using plastic wrap, shape the dough into a 2 1/2-inch-diameter log. Discard the wrap. Press the chopped almonds into the surface of the log and cover with another piece of plastic wrap. Place the cookie dough log in the refrigerator for 1 hour. You can also freeze the dough for up to 4 weeks and bake the cookies later.

Remove the dough from the refrigerator and remove the plastic wrap. Using a sharp knife, slice the log into 1/4-inch-thick cookie rounds. Place the cookies on a nonstick cookie sheet and bake for 12 minutes, or until golden brown. Remove from the oven and cool completely on a wire rack before serving.

Fall Berry Fool

My Granny Harris used to make my brother and me Gooseberry Fool as a treat whenever we were especially well-behaved. This is my version of her recipe—blackberries stand in for the gooseberries. I associate this dessert with a crisp fall day.

{ Serves 6 }
10 cups blackberries
1 1/2 cups superfine sugar
1 1/2 cups heavy cream
1 cup mascarpone cheese

In a heavy-bottomed saucepan, heat the blackberries and the sugar over low heat. Simmer, stirring constantly, until the sugar has melted and the juice of the berries is syrupy, about 20 minutes.

Push the mixture through a fine-mesh sieve, squeezing out as much of the juice as possible from the berry pulp. Discard the berry pulp. Chill the blackberry syrup in the refrigerator.

In a large bowl using an electric mixer, beat the heavy cream until soft peaks form. Soften the mascarpone by beating it with a wooden spoon, then gently fold in the whipped cream with a metal spoon. Add 1 1/2 cups of the blackberry syrup to the cheese-cream mixture and stir until marbled. Using tumblers as serving bowls, place a tablespoonful of the cheese-cream mixture in the bottom and then layer a spoonful of the berry syrup on top. Alternate a layer of the cheese-cream mixture with berry syrup until each tumbler is full, creating a pleasing striped effect. Transfer the filled tumblers to the refrigerator and chill for a minimum of 3 hours for the fool to get firm. Garnish with blackberries and serve with a couple of Almond Cookies (see recipe on page 41).

THE OUTCOME

The ritual of dining with close friends is a scene that has played out since time immemorial—as comfortable as between the pages of a Regency novel or a Bridget Jones's dinner party. Our evening contained all the necessary components—a table of favorite foods and friends. To create the mood, we lit a nineteenth-century candle-filled chandelier and made a blazing log fire. During the cocktail hour, we lingered over mouthfuls of sweet and salty bacon-wrapped dates and scallops while sipping gin. Then, leisurely moving to the dinner table, we savored the warm Favorite Chicken and Mushroom Pie, enjoying mouthfuls of crisp buttery pastry and soothing gravy. We finished with a delightfully light berry fool. The evening was a success—our simple-supper guests were cosseted and comfortable in this cozy enclave. Finally, they left satisfied in the crisp autumnal night air.

RIGHT: Depression-glass stands display beautiful marbled Fall Berry Foul and Almond Cookies.

anniversary dinner

APPETIZERS

Roasted Beet, Blood Orange, and
    Watercress Salad with Boucheron
    Crostini
Fettuccine with Minted Tomato Sauce

MAIN DISHES

Roasted White and Green Asparagus
Salt-Crust Baked Salmon
Salsa Verde
Balsamic-Glazed Cipollini Onions

DESSERT

Lemon Caramelized Apple
    Frangipane

SERVES 12

LEFT: Toasting my husband, Buck, at the start of our anniversary fete.

An anniversary dinner is the perfect event to make an annual affair. Steeped in the nostalgia of the past—not just a remembrance of a binding event—it is a reunion to share with those friends who cannot get together more often. This occasion is the perfect excuse to join the old and the new, the past and the present, both those who attended the original celebration along with new extended friends and family.

Michael and I threw this celebratory dinner party to commemorate Buck's and my third wedding anniversary. What better person to collaborate on such a meaningful event than our close friend Michael? He always is in sync with our culinary and visual aesthetics. The party was held at Sonia and Daniel's fabulous loft in lower Manhattan during the height of spring. We marked the freshness of the season by bringing in a garden full of flowers in a spectrum of purple shades. Close friends dined with us at a huge six-foot-long antique table elegantly set with heirloom silver and linens suitable for such a special occasion.

THE LOOK

Sonia and Daniel's loft, with grand proportions comparable to a large country house, is filled with furniture that would overpower a smaller space. The large antiques play off against a backdrop of modern photography and soothing, muted wall colors. Our guests were dressed smartly in black and white—boys donning cardigans, jackets, and ties and girls in exquisite silk dresses. Mirroring the colors of the floral arrangements, we chose lilac linen napkins with picot edging, which were laid next to the family silver and white porcelain plates.

THE MOOD

Music
For an anniversary celebration, the choice of background music should be anything that reminds you of the original event and is particularly meaningful to both you and your friends.

Lighting
We clustered several tea lights in simple glass votives among the floral arrangements on the table. Softly illuminating the flowers, the tea lights also cast romantic shadows around the room. Dimming the lights further fostered an intimate mood.

Flowers
We arranged purple hydrangeas, parrot tulips, classic lilacs, lavender hyacinths, purple ranunculus, and pink jasmine vines in frosted-glass cylinders. Make up bouquets in your hand, then cut the stems the same length to fit the vessels. After placing the flowers in the vases, fill in the gaps with individual blooms. Then pour in enough water to cover the stems.

Invitation
For an event as important as an anniversary dinner, we love the formality of a written invitation sent in the mail.

THE PLAN

The day before

/ Compile to-do lists.
/ Shop for all ingredients.
/ Make the Lemon Caramelized Apple Frangipane and refrigerate.
/ Toast the walnuts for the Fettuccine with Minted Tomato Sauce.
/ Prepare the Salsa Verde.
/ Make up the dressing for the Roasted Beet, Blood Orange, and Watercress Salad with Boucheron Crostini.
/ Make up the floral arrangement as described on the previous page.

The morning of

/ Lay out serving pieces and glassware, and set the table.
/ Chill bottles of white wine.
/ Prepare the crust for the Salt-Crust Baked Salmon and coat the fish.
/ Cook the Minted Tomato Sauce, but do not add the walnuts until the last minute.
/ Prepare the white and green asparagus.
/ Drizzle the onions with oil and vinegar for the Balsamic-Glazed Cipollini Onions.
/ Make the pasta to go with the Fettuccine with Minted Tomato Sauce.

Last minute

/ Bake the salt-crust salmon when guests sit down for the first course.
/ Roast the balsamic glazed cipollini onions.
/ Roast the white and green asparagus.
/ Prepare the Roasted Beet, Blood Orange, and Watercress Salad with Boucheron Crostini.
/ Put the pasta on to boil for the Fettuccine with Minted Tomato Sauce.
/ Heat the Minted Tomato Sauce and serve with walnuts over the freshly cooked pasta immediately.
/ Plate the food.

CHEATS

The floral arrangements that we chose could be quite time-consuming, especially because so many are needed to create the desired effect. So, the first cheat would be to turn to a trusted florist to make up the arrangements as per your specifications. This is the only occasion where there are only a few shortcuts to the recipes. Don't be daunted by these seemingly complicated dishes because they are much easier than they appear. The only food cheat is to buy a good-quality fettuccine from an Italian grocer instead of making it from scratch. A foolproof recipe, the salmon coated with a salt crust cooks evenly without drying out and can be left alone as it bakes. The crust also cuts down on cleaning time, as the salt keeps all the juices in the fish and off the oven surface.

anniversary dinner

Roasted Beet, Blood Orange, and Watercress Salad with Boucheron Crostini

The combination of a citrus-flavored salad dressing with a crusty cheese crostini accompaniment is scrumptious. When peeling and slicing beets, always wear rubber gloves to prevent the juice from coloring your fingers.

{ *Serves 12* }
36 baby beets (mix of red, pink, and yellow)
2 cups walnut halves
6 blood oranges
1/3 cup aged sherry vinegar
2/3 cup extra virgin olive oil
1/2 teaspoon runny honey
1 teaspoon coarse sea salt
1 teaspoon freshly ground black pepper
2 baguettes, cut into 1/2-inch-thick slices
Twelve 1/8-inch-thick slices boucheron cheese
4 bunches watercress

Preheat the oven to 400°F.

Remove the beet tops and tails and place in a roasting pan. Bake for 40 minutes, or until the beets are tender. Reduce the oven temperature to 325°F. Leave the beets to cool, then peel and thinly slice them.

Place the walnuts on a baking sheet, transfer to the oven, and toast for 15 minutes, or until lightly browned. Remove from the oven and set aside. Leave the oven on.

Zest and juice 2 of the oranges, place the zest and juice in a bowl, and mix with the vinegar, oil, honey, salt, and pepper. Peel the remaining oranges with a knife, removing the white pith along with the peel. Supreme the segments by slicing between the membranes and releasing the flesh.

Place the baguette slices on a baking sheet, transfer to the oven, and toast for 5 minutes, or until golden brown. Lay a slice of boucheron over the bread slices, return to the oven, and bake for another 2 minutes. Remove from the oven and set aside.

Arrange the watercress in a large salad bowl and drizzle with the dressing. Toss to coat the leaves. Plate individual servings of watercress, beets, and orange segments, and scatter the toasted walnut halves over the top. Lay a crostini next to the mound of salad and serve immediately.

LEFT: The Roasted Beet, Blood Orange, and Watercress Salad appetizer is served on a contemporary chinoiserie Wedgwood plate.

Fettuccine with Minted Tomato Sauce

This incredibly light tomato sauce can be served with a variety of dishes, from pasta to a fish stew.

{ *Serves 12* }
2 tablespoons extra virgin olive oil
1 1/2 red onions, finely chopped
2 teaspoons flaked sea salt
2 teaspoons freshly ground black pepper
2 pinches peperoncino
Two 28-ounce cans San Marzano Italian whole plum tomatoes in tomato puree
1 bunch basil leaves, cut into chiffonade
1 bunch mint leaves, cut into chiffonade
1 cup walnuts
1 tablespoon coarse sea salt
Fresh Fettuccine (recipe follows) or two 17 1/2-ounce packages imported dried fettuccine
1/2 cup freshly grated Parmigiano-Reggiano, plus 1 cup for serving

In a large saucepan, heat the oil over medium heat and sauté the onions until softened, about 5 minutes. Add the flaked sea salt, pepper, and peperoncino. Roughly cut the tomatoes with kitchen shears and pour them, along with the tomato puree, into the saucepan of onions. Stir the onions and tomatoes to combine and add a handful of basil and a handful of mint. Lower the heat and leave the sauce to simmer.

In a large skillet over medium heat, toast the walnuts until lightly browned, about 5 minutes. Remove from the heat and set aside.

Fill a large pot with water and the coarse sea salt. Bring to a boil and add the pasta. Cover and bring back to boil. Stir once and leave to cook; fresh pasta will take 2 to 3 minutes, and dried pasta will take approximately 10 minutes. Drain the cooked pasta, and stir it through the sauce. Sprinkle with the cheese, walnuts, and remaining mint and basil. Serve immediately.

Fresh Fettuccine

Making pasta with a pasta machine is one of those tasks that is extremely relaxing if time is not an issue and stressful if rushed. So do allow about two hours to prepare the fettuccine—it is worth it.

{ *Serves 12* }
4 cups Italian durum or all-purpose flour
6 medium eggs
1 tablespoon olive oil
1 pinch fine sea salt

On a clean work surface, make a mound of flour and form a well in the middle. Crack the eggs into the well and lightly beat with a fork. Scoop a little flour from the outer edges of the mound and draw upward, allowing flour from the top to fall into the well. Using your fingertips, combine the flour with the eggs and mix well. Stretch the dough out and fold it back on itself. Add the oil and salt and knead for 5 minutes.

Cover the dough with plastic wrap and set aside for 10 minutes to soften. Divide the dough into 4 pieces. Work on one piece at a time. Cover the other pieces in plastic wrap. Shape the

Fresh Fettuccine recipe continues pg. 54

RIGHT: Bowls of homemade fettuccine, dressed with tomato sauce, ready to serve.

anniversary dinner

anniversary dinner

Fresh Fettuccine
continued

pasta dough into a patty 1/4 inch thick and feed through the pasta machine on the widest, thickest setting (gauge number 1). Allow the dough to feed through on its own without forcing or pulling it. Once passed through, fold the dough in half and pass through again. Repeat this process 4 more times before switching the pasta machine to the next lower setting (gauge number 2). Feed through the dough before folding, then repeat the process 4 more times. Switch the pasta machine to the next setting (gauge number 3), fold the dough, and pass through 3 times. If the pasta becomes too long to handle, cut the dough in half widthwise and continue to process the halves individually. Pass the dough through the pasta rollers once on a lower setting (gauge number 4) and again on gauge number 5. Lay the pasta sheets on a wire rack and repeat this process for each of the remaining pasta dough patties.

Change the rollers on the pasta machine to fettuccine cutters and pass each of the pasta sheets through one at a time. Lay the strands of pasta on a wire rack or hang on a wire coat hanger until ready to use.

MAIN DISHES

Roasted White and Green Asparagus

This versatile dish can be served hot or at room temperature. It is a great accompaniment to a variety of dishes, such as grilled meat or fish.

{ Serves 12 }
2 bunches white asparagus
2 bunches green asparagus
Zest of 1 lemon
6 tablespoons extra virgin olive oil
2 teaspoons flaked sea salt
2 teaspoons freshly ground black pepper
1/2 cup finely chopped Italian parsley

Preheat the oven to 450°F.

Remove the tough part of the asparagus stalks and arrange on a baking sheet in a single layer.

In a small bowl, combine the lemon zest and oil. Drizzle the asparagus with the oil mixture and season with the salt and pepper. Place in the oven and roast for 5 minutes, or until the asparagus is tender, tossing once so it cooks evenly. Remove from the oven, sprinkle with the parsley, and serve.

Salt-Crust Baked Salmon

When you cook a large whole salmon, it can easily dry out. However, a salt crust seals in the natural juices to keep its flavor and create a moist texture.

{ Serves 12 }
4 pounds coarse sea salt
4 large eggs, beaten
One 4-pound whole salmon, gutted and cleaned
1 lemon, thinly sliced
1 bunch thyme leaves
1 bunch basil leaves, cut into chiffonade
1 bunch sage leaves, cut into chiffonade
Salt-Crust Baked Salmon recipe continues on pg. 57

PREVIOUS SPREAD: *From left to right, clockwise:* Our romantic table scape includes masses of flowers and flickering votives. A whole baked salmon with a salt crust. RIGHT: Roasted White and Green Asparagus tightly packed into a narrow terrine.

Salt-Crust Baked Salmon

Preheat the oven to 350°F.

In a large glass bowl, stir together the salt and eggs until the mixture resembles wet sand. Line a large baking sheet with aluminum foil and lay out a 1 1/2-inch-thick layer of salt. Place the salmon on top of the salt. Line the cavity of the fish with lemon slices and fill with the herbs. Be careful not to overstuff. The top and bottom slices of fish should meet up. Cover the salmon with the remaining salt and egg mixture, place in the oven, and bake for 45 to 55 minutes, until tender.

Remove from the oven and take off the crust immediately so the fish does not continue to bake. Discard the lemon and herbs. Peel back the skin and transfer the top half of the salmon onto a serving platter. Remove the spine and bones, discard them, and transfer the bottom half of the fish onto the platter. Serve immediately.

Salsa Verde

This salty, aromatic salsa is the perfect accompaniment to fish. We like to make up a large batch, and any that is not used can be frozen for up to three months.

{ Makes 1 cup}
1 bunch Italian parsley
1 bunch basil leaves
1 bunch mint leaves
1/3 cup salt-covered capers, washed and drained
4 anchovy fillets
1/2 cup extra virgin olive oil
1 teaspoon Dijon mustard (preferably Grey Poupon)
2 tablespoons aged sherry vinegar
1 teaspoon freshly ground black pepper

In a food processor, combine the herbs, capers, anchovies, and 1/4 cup of the oil. Process until a paste is formed.

In large bowl, whisk the remaining 1/4 cup of oil with the mustard, vinegar, and pepper. Add the paste and thoroughly combine. If not using right away, cover and refrigerate until ready to use.

Balsamic-Glazed Cipollini Onions

We love the play of sharp and sweet—the combination of sweet cipollini onions with sharp balsamic vinegar is a match made in gastronomic heaven.

{ Serves 12 }
36 cipollini onions, peeled
1/4 cup extra virgin olive oil
1/2 cup aged balsamic vinegar
2 teaspoons flaked sea salt
2 teaspoons freshly ground black pepper

Preheat the oven to 400°F.

Place the onions on a large baking sheet and drizzle with the oil and vinegar. Season with the salt and pepper. These steps can be done in advance and the baking sheet set aside. Place in the oven and roast for 30 minutes, or until tender. Remove from the oven and serve immediately.

LEFT: A filigree bowl of Balsamic-Glazed Cipollini Onions garnished with sprigs of thyme.

Lemon Caramelized Apple Frangipane

This dessert can be made with or without pastry. If you use pastry, it becomes a tart. We prefer the frangipane served as a pudding without the tart crust. Either way, it can be made a day in advance and reheated before serving or enjoyed cold. Twelve pastry rings are needed.

{ Serves 12 }
Zest and juice of 1 1/2 lemons
3 pounds Bramley or Braeburn apples, peeled, cored, and sliced
1 1/2 cups brown sugar
1 1/2 cups (3 sticks) unsalted butter, softened
1 3/4 cups superfine sugar
6 large eggs
2 cups ground almonds

Preheat the oven to 350°F. Butter the pastry rings and a cookie sheet.

In a large saucepan, combine the lemon juice and zest with the apples and brown sugar. Place over medium heat and cook until the apples have softened, about 5 minutes. Drain the apple slices and arrange in the bottom of the pastry rings.

In a large metal bowl, cream the butter and superfine sugar with a wooden spoon. Beat the eggs into the butter and sugar mixture one at a time until thoroughly combined. Using a metal spoon, lightly fold in the ground almonds and spoon over the apples.

Place in the oven and bake for 1 hour, or until the cakes are golden on top and a skewer inserted into the middle comes out clean. Remove from the oven and let rest for 10 minutes, then arrange each pudding on individual plates. Use a spatula to remove them from the pastry rings.

THE OUTCOME

This anniversary celebration was an opportunity for Michael and me to show our friends, and of course my husband, how much we love and appreciate them. We strove to create a fantasy world of beauty in the wonderful loft space, with perfect floral arrangements, lighting, fine wines, and delightful food. Our group, clad in exquisite outfits, dined on course after glorious course—from the tender Salt-Crust Baked Salmon, to the salty sharp freshness of the Salsa Verde, to the creamy goat cheese crostini. By serving the dinner Italian-style, with the pasta course followed by fish, the meal was surprisingly light, leaving just enough room to finish with the sticky-sweet Lemon Caramelized Apple Frangipane. We thoroughly enjoyed this very special gathering and promised to make it a yearly event.

RIGHT: Frangipane served on a mother-of-pearl plate.

blissful beach picnic

SERVES 8

LEFT: Ruffled raffia umbrellas form a makeshift cabana for a beach picnic.

One glorious weekend in early September found Michael and me as the happy guests of Charlotte and Douglas's South Hampton beach retreat. Their home is a perfect Long Island clapboard house, nestled among sand dunes and gazing out to sea, the ideal spot for a blissful beach picnic.

A truly perfect day at the beach should be a happy marriage of laid-back ease with meticulous planning. You are transporting not only the food but also your home comforts in a bid to create the casual insouciance of a seasoned beach picnicker. However, the flip side is that once successfully camped, there is little else to do but bask in the glow of the sunshine and the admiration of your well-fed, contented guests.

THE LOOK

Surrounded by natural beach beauty, we chose neutral colors and heavy textures that blend with the background. Our West Elm jute rug provided not only a cover to sit on but also a much-needed thick barrier to keep food sand-free. When spending a full day at the beach, it is also essential to offer shade from the midday sun—vital for picnickers and the food alike. We achieved this with a homemade cabana made up of three large white-fringed umbrellas which mimicked the waves and kept the sun at bay.

We dressed in keeping with our beach-themed party, opting for casual, nautical-inspired tops teemed up with white wide-legged sailor pants, jeans, and shorts. As far as etiquette goes, when lunching on the beach, it is considerate to wear something a little more than simply a string bikini or pair of board shorts (worse still, a pair of Speedos!).

THE MOOD

Music

As the beach is a public place, it is inconsiderate to impose your music on other beachgoers. Apart from anything else, nothing is more relaxing than the sound of the crashing waves.

Lighting

Candles are superfluous during daytime. However, should you wish to linger on after the sun has set, garden candles with their bamboo wind visors are ideal. The long bamboo sticks can be pushed deep into the sand to keep them upright.

Food, containers, and flatware

In an age when we should all be more environmentally conscious, there are many wood and paper options for containing food. These also happen to be far more aesthetically pleasing than their plastic counterparts. We picked items from Ripplecups, a producer of bamboo tableware that offers pretty, disposable bamboo cutlery sets along with reed molded bowls, plates, and cups as a picnic set. We carried food to and from the beach in medium-size cardboard boxes, and used lacquered wood plates to complement our eco-friendly flatware. Though glassware is by far the nicest option for outdoor dining, when at the beach it is essential to leave all glassware at home.

It takes just one breakage for glass shards to be lost in the sand, only to be painfully discovered by some unsuspecting beachgoer. We recommend that you tidy up at regular intervals during the party to deter guests in the form of flies, wasps, and seagulls. Prevent plates and cutlery from being blown across the sand by using beach stones to secure them.

Invitation

A day at the beach can be as informal as you wish, with a call or e-mail to set arrangements in place. Should you wish to send an invitation, a selection of vintage seaside postcards would be charming.

THE PLAN

The day before

/ Compile to-do lists.
/ Check the weather report.
/ Go to the local grocery store and farmers' market to buy all the ingredients.
/ For Jane Muss's Dried Fruit and Mint Tea Salad, soak the dried fruit in cold mint tea overnight.
/ Boil the balsamic vinegar to create the reduction for the Fresh Figs with Parmesan and Balsamic Glaze.
/ Prepare the Veal Meatloaf and refrigerate.
/ Make the Onion, Eggplant, and Sweet Pepper Confit.
/ Make the Bulgur Wheat Salad, adding the tomatoes right before serving.
/ Prepare all salad dressings.
/ Pack suntan lotion, rugs, cushions, umbrellas, and garden candles.
/ Pack paper flatware, cutlery, and paper cups.

The morning of

/ Prepare and roast the Roasted Autumn Vegetables.
/ Make the End of Summer Corn and Shrimp Salad, but do not add the corn and basil until the last minute.
/ Grate the beets and carrot for Susan's Grated Beet and Apple Salad.
/ Mix up the Cinnamon Crème Fraîche and keep chilled in the icebox.
/ Make the Hot Mulled Cider and transfer to thermoses.
/ Pack up the car.

Last minute

/ Set out rugs, umbrellas, and cushions on the beach.
/ Grate the apples for Susan's Grated Beet and Apple Salad.
/ Complete the Fresh Figs with Parmesan and Balsamic Glaze.
/ Toss salads with the dressings.
/ Lay out plates, cutlery, napkins, and cups.

CHEATS

Jane Muss's Dried Fruit and Mint Tea Salad is a "cheat," as you only need to pour luke-warm tea over dried fruits to create this dish. If you do not have the time to reduce the balsamic vinegar, the easy alternative is to use a good-quality balsamic syrup.

Though the beach picnic involves quite a lot of preplanning, the beauty is that there is barely any effort once you arrive, and better still no cleaning up beyond putting all the rubbish and plates in the bin.

blissful beach picnic

Hot Mulled Cider

When the chill of the evening sets in, this drink is a warming welcome. Kept in a thermos, the cider will keep hot all day long.

{ Serves 8 }
1 cup raw brown sugar
4 1/2 quarts apple cider
2 teaspoons ground allspice
1 teaspoon freshly grated nutmeg
2 teaspoons ground ginger
Juice and zest of 1 orange
2 cinnamon sticks
2 teaspoons whole cloves, tied in cheesecloth

In a large saucepan, combine the sugar and cider and slowly bring to a boil over medium heat, whisking to dissolve the sugar. Add the rest of the ingredients and simmer for 20 minutes. Remove the cinnamon sticks and the bag of cloves and immediately transfer to thermoses.

MAIN DISHES

Onion, Eggplant, and Sweet Pepper Confit

Michael invented this delicious confit as a condiment for his Veal Meatloaf.

{Makes 3 cups}
3 Roasted Red Peppers (recipe follows), cut into 1-inch cubes
1 medium eggplant, peeled and cut into 1-inch cubes
1 small red onion, coarsely chopped
4 garlic cloves, minced
One 28-ounce can San Marzano tomatoes, drained and coarsely chopped
1/4 cup extra virgin olive oil
1/2 teaspoon peperoncino
1/2 teaspoon kosher salt
1/2 teaspoon freshly ground black pepper

Preheat the oven to 400°F. Grease a baking sheet and set aside.

In a large bowl, combine all the ingredients. Place on the greased baking sheet, transfer to the oven, and roast until the vegetables are very tender, about 1 hour. Remove from the oven and serve at room temperature.

Roasted Red Peppers

Roasted red peppers are so versatile that they can be used in a wide variety of dishes, such as meatloaf, as we do here, stuffed with cheese and couscous, or served cold in salads. They can also be made into a savory marmalade. The best time to buy red peppers is at the end of summer or early fall.

{Makes 5 roasted peppers}
5 red bell peppers

Grip a pepper in a pair of tongs and hold directly over a gas flame, turning until the skin is blackened and blistered. Once all the peppers have been roasted, place them in a sealed plastic bag to steam for 5 minutes. When cooled, peel and seed.

LEFT: Lunch is served in chic disposable paper containers.

End of Summer Corn and Shrimp Salad

Do not be tempted to cheat and add a can of corn kernels, as it is the crunch of the uncooked corn kernels that makes this salad so fantastic. The corn kernels are easily removed by running a sharp knife away from you down the cob.

{ Serves 8 }
32 large shrimp, peeled and deveined
2 tablespoons crab boil
3/4 cup extra virgin olive oil
2 tablespoons Dijon mustard (preferably Grey Poupon)
3 tablespoons sherry vinegar
1 tablespoon finely chopped shallots
3 tablespoons chopped chives
3 cups fresh corn kernels (or 8 ears of corn)
2 tablespoons fresh basil, cut into chiffonade

Place the shrimp and crab boil in a large saucepan and cover with water. Place over medium-high heat and bring to a boil; cook for about ten minutes, or until the shrimp are just pink. Turn off the heat and allow the shrimp to cool in the cooking liquid.

In a small glass jar, combine the oil, mustard, vinegar, shallots, and chives. Secure the lid of the jar tightly and shake well until combined.

Drain the shrimp and place in a large bowl. Pour the dressing over the shrimp, cover with plastic wrap, and refrigerate for 1 hour. When ready to serve, add the corn kernels and basil to the shrimp and toss together.

Roasted Autumn Vegetables

This side dish can be served at room temperature or hot. If the vegetables are an accompaniment to salad, make sure they cool down before serving; otherwise the lettuce will wilt.

{ Serves 8 }
1 butternut squash, peeled, seeded, and cut into 1-inch cubes
3 yams, peeled and cut into 1-inch cubes
5 carrots, cut into 1-inch rounds
4 parsnips, cut into 1-inch rounds
1 large turnip, peeled and cut into 1-inch cubes
1 red onion, coarsely chopped
2 sprigs rosemary
2 sprigs thyme
1/4 cup extra virgin olive oil
1 teaspoon kosher salt
1 teaspoon freshly ground black pepper

Preheat the oven to 400°F.

Combine all the vegetables and herbs in a large bowl, toss with the oil to coat, then add the salt and pepper and toss to coat. Transfer to a large baking dish, place in the oven, and roast for 1 hour, or until the vegetables are tender. Remove from the oven and serve hot or at room temperature.

RIGHT: Two lacquer trays lined with leaves from the garden hold Fresh Figs with Parmesan and Balsamic Glaze.

blissful beach picnic

Fresh Figs with Parmesan and Balsamic Glaze

Although the balsamic vinegar takes time to reduce, it is well worth the effort. The balsamic glaze will keep for up to a week in a sealed glass jar.

{ Serves 8 }
8 fresh, ripe black figs
1/2 cup balsamic vinegar
1/2 cup Parmesan cheese shavings

Slice the figs in half lengthwise and set aside. Pour the balsamic vinegar into a small saucepan and simmer over medium heat until it has reduced by half and is syrupy, approximately 30 minutes. Dot the figs with the warm syrup and sprinkle the Parmesan shavings on top just before serving.

Veal Meatloaf

This quintessentially American dish is perfect for a picnic as it travels so well. Keep cool on ice until ready to serve.

{ Serves 8 }
1 tablespoon extra virgin olive oil
1 cup minced onion
1 cup finely chopped celery
1 garlic clove, minced
1/2 pound mushrooms, finely chopped
1/4 cup finely chopped Italian parsley
2 Roasted Red Peppers (see recipe on page 65), roughly chopped
1 1/2 pounds ground veal
1/2 cup fresh breadcrumbs
1 large egg, beaten
1 1/2 teaspoons flaked sea salt
1 1/2 teaspoons coarsely ground black pepper
1 teaspoon freshly grated nutmeg

Preheat the oven to 375°F.

In a sauté pan, heat the oil over medium heat and add the onion and celery. Cook until softened, about 5 minutes. Add the garlic and mushrooms and continue to cook until there is no liquid left in the pan, about 5 minutes. Turn off the heat and add the parsley and roasted peppers. Set aside to cool.

In a large bowl, thoroughly combine the veal, breadcrumbs, and egg along with the salt, pepper, and nutmeg. Stir in the roasted pepper mixture.

Transfer the meat mixture to a 4 by 5-inch loaf pan and shape into a loaf. Set the pan into a large baking dish. Pour boiling water into the baking dish, about 1 inch high. Bake for 1 hour and 15 minutes, or until cooked through. Remove from oven and let cool. To turn the meatloaf out of the pan, run a knife around the edges to loosen, then invert the loaf onto a serving platter.

LEFT: Veal Meatloaf sliced and served on a bamboo cutting board.

blissful beach picnic

Bulgur Wheat Salad

This is a great summer staple, which makes a particularly delicious barbeque accompaniment. You can substitute brown rice for the bulgur wheat.

{ Serves 8 }
2 cups bulgur wheat
8 cups boiling water
1 cucumber, peeled, cut in half, seeded, and diced
1/2 cup minced scallions, white and green parts
1/4 cup finely chopped fresh mint
1/3 cup extra virgin olive oil
Juice of 1 lemon
1 pinch flaked sea salt
1/4 teaspoon freshly ground black pepper
2 tomatoes, peeled, seeded, and coarsely chopped (see Tomato Water technique on page 164)

Place the bulgur wheat in a large glass bowl and pour in the boiling water. Cover with plastic wrap and set aside for 3 hours. Drain the bulgur wheat of any remaining liquid and transfer to a serving bowl. Add the cucumber, scallions, and mint.

In a small bowl, whisk together the olive oil, lemon juice, salt, and pepper. Pour over the salad and mix well. Cover the salad and refrigerate until ready to serve. Just before serving, drain the chopped tomatoes and add to the salad; stir thoroughly.

Susan's Grated Beet and Apple Salad

A good trick when handling beets is to wear rubber gloves, especially when grating, so as to avoid the telltale red hand.

{ Serves 8 }
3 large beets, trimmed and peeled
2 Granny Smith apples, peeled and cored
2 carrots
1/4 cup extra virgin olive oil
1/4 cup balsamic vinegar
1 teaspoon kosher salt
1 teaspoon freshly ground black pepper
2 tablespoons fresh basil, cut into chiffonade

Using a box grater, grate the beets, apples, and carrots and place in a large bowl.

In a small glass jar, combine the oil, vinegar, salt, pepper, and basil. Shake vigorously and pour over the vegetables. Toss the vegetables and serve immediately.

PREVIOUS SPREAD: Enjoying our sundrenched picnic, including Jane Muss's Dried Fruit and Mint Tea Salad.

Jane Muss's Dried Fruit and Mint Tea Salad

This fruit salad, invented by my best friend's mother, is divinely simple and delicious.

{ Serves 8 }
2 mint tea bags (or 1 large bunch fresh mint)
1 cup dried cranberries
1 cup dried cherries
1 cup dried plums
2 cups dried apricots
1 cup golden raisins
8 star anise
3 cinnamon sticks
4 whole cloves

Brew 4 cups of mint tea with the tea bags or fresh mint for 6 minutes and let cool. Strain.

In a large glass bowl, place all the remaining ingredients and cover with the strained and cooled tea. Cover and refrigerate overnight. You will not need to add any sugar as the fruits have enough natural sweetness. By morning the fruits will be sitting in a puddle of delicious spiced syrup.

Cinnamon Crème Fraîche

This lightly spiced cream is the perfect accompaniment to Jane Muss's Dried Fruit and Mint Tea Salad. Ice cream also works well.

{ Serves 8 }
2 cups crème fraîche
1 tablespoon ground cinnamon
2 tablespoons superfine sugar, or as desired

In a medium bowl, thoroughly mix the crème fraîche and cinnamon together. Add the sugar, cover, and refrigerate until ready to serve.

THE OUTCOME

Our glorious picnic at the beach was worth every effort—we lounged like kings and queens in our handcrafted cabana. Under the morning sun, we cavorted with child like abadon on the sand and in the sea, until overcome with a longing for luscious food. The fresh flavors of crisp corn and shrimp salad complemented the rich texture of Michael's Veal Meatloaf, which was washed down with the subtle spiced Hot Mulled Cider. Dusk found us sated, relaxed, and cider-warmed. With blankets around our shoulders, we watched as the sun sank slowly into the sea.

family lunch

COCKTAILS
COCKTAILS
Homemade Pimms
Homemade Lemonade

APPETIZER
My Mum's Lemon and
    Goat Cheese Soufflés

MAIN DISHES
Butterflied and Grilled
    Cornish Game Hens

Spicy Peaches
Layered Salad with Roasted
    Tomatoes and Lemon-and-
    Caper Dressing

DESSERT
American-style Eton Mess

SERVES 10

LEFT: A delicious family lunch on my aunt and uncle's front lawn.

Deep in the heart of the Gloucestershire countryside, Gay and Conrad's neo-Gothic cottage was the setting for a summer Sunday lunch thrown to welcome Michael and his mother, Marie, to England. We brought together my mother, Gina, in-laws Philip and Pat, and cousins Tommy, Ricky, and Katie to meet the Levas at my aunt and uncle's house. A family gathering can be overwhelming, so we chose a simple lunch of our favorite foods to keep the day stress-free. Pulling my aunt's old oak table onto the lawn and assembling chairs from the garden, we found respite from the relentless heat in the shadows cast by the house. The scene we set was simple, and we mismatched the furniture to emphasize the casual nature of the affair. If the weather is beautiful, anyone can bring together odd pieces of furniture outside at the last minute to make for an easy, relaxed style.

Unaccustomed to endless days of sunshine, the British flock outdoors at the first peep of a sunny day. If the weather is good, then there is truly no nicer place to throw a family lunch than outdoors in the fresh air. And so, amid the purples and greens of lavender and lawn, we served family favorites, beginning with my mother's Lemon and Goat Cheese Soufflés and finishing with an Eton Mess updated with an American twist in honor of our guests.

THE LOOK

Family get-togethers can be stressful, so aim to make the day relaxing, beginning with your outfits. We set a balance between casual and smart—comfortable enough to be able to run about but smart enough to set the tone of this celebratory occasion. My aunt's Elizabethan oak table was dressed down with a variety of weathered garden chairs and benches.

THE MOOD

Music
We did without music because it would have drowned out the natural sounds of Gay's garden and the lively conversation.

Lighting
Pulling the table into the shade created the perfect lighting and provided us with a and comfortable temperature throughout the day. No additional light was needed.

Flowers
My mother, a wildflower enthusiast, foraged the hedgerows and fields for a simple and verdant arrangement. We made low arrangements for the table so as not to obstruct the view

of the seated guests. While wildflowers are lovely; you must be careful to avoid plants known to cause allergies or that drop excessive pollen.

Invitation

There is no need for formal invitations for a family affair. E-mails and phone calls are the best way to organize such a casual event.

THE PLAN

The day before

/ Compile to-do lists.
/ Shop for all ingredients.
/ Assign responsibilities to each family member.
/ Make the Borage Ice Cubes.
/ Make lemon syrup for the Homemade Lemonade.
/ Make the Lemon-and-Caper Dressing.
/ Bake the meringue for the American-style Eton Mess.
/ Cook the lentils for the Layered Salad.

The morning of

/ Pull the table onto the lawn.
/ Lay out serving pieces and glassware, and set the table.
/ Pick and arrange wildflowers.
/ Make the Homemade Pimms mix.
/ Prepare the lentil mixture for the Layered Salad.
/ Prepare the Roasted Tomatoes.
/ Make up My Mum's Lemon and Goat Cheese Soufflés.
/ For the Spicy Peaches, blanch and peel the peaches and coat with lemon juice.
/ Rinse and butterfly the game hens for the Butterflied and Grilled Cornish Game Hens and marinate in olive oil and herbs.

Last minute

/ Make up the Homemade Pimms and Homemade Lemonade in large pitchers and refrigerate.
/ Bake My Mum's Lemon and Goat Cheese Soufflés.
/ Assemble the Layered Salad and top with Roasted Tomatoes.
/ For the Spicy Peaches, slice the peaches and add the spices.
/ Grill the hens for the Butterflied and Grilled Cornish Game Hens.
/ Whip the cream and make the American-style Eton mess.

CHEATS

It is important to cheat wherever you feel necessary to keep the day as stress-free as possible. Most of our recipes can be prepared a day before, enabling you to relax and enjoy time with your family. Our Homemade Lemonade recipe is easy and can be prepped in advance, but you can buy sparkling lemonade for the Homemade Pimms. Most people do not make their own Pimms and in fact use an over-the-counter version. There is no shame if you wish to follow suit; however, it is great to be able to impress everyone with the original recipe. As a time-saver, My Mum's Lemon and Goat Cheese Soufflés may be placed in the freezer after they have been baked and are set until needed. Once thoroughly defrosted, sprinkle with goat cheese on top and bake again for 20 to 25 minutes, until they have risen and are golden brown on top. Humidity can wreak havoc when trying to achieve the perfect meringue. This is important to bear in mind when deciding whether to cheat or not. Michael is a fan of premade meringues, whereas I always make my own. If you have a trusted baker, then by all means buy their handmade version. But if there was ever a time to attempt a meringue, then this is the recipe, because it does not matter if it cracks. You will be breaking the meringue into pieces anyway.

Homemade Pimms

Pimms is a quintessentially English summer cocktail, synonymous with outdoor entertaining. A garden party is not complete without a few pitchers of Pimms gracing the table. I was given the recipe for this version by a barman in Devon, England. Do not skimp on the garnish.

{ Serves 10 }
3 1/2 ounces sweet sherry or port
7 ounces red vermouth
10 ounces gin
3 1/2 ounces Cointreau
2 1/2 quarts Homemeade Lemonade (recipe follows)
Ice cubes, preferably Borage Ice Cubes (see recipe on page 80)

For the garnish
10 sprigs mint
1/2 cucumber, thinly sliced
Handful of strawberries, quartered
1/2 orange, thinly sliced
1/2 lemon, thinly sliced

In a large pitcher, mix the sherry, vermouth, gin, and Cointreau. To make the basic Pimms mix, add 4 parts lemonade to 1 part Pimms. (If you do not have a large enough pitcher to accommodate the Pimms-Lemonade mixture, keep the Pimms mix in the refrigerator and make up individual glasses as needed.)

Fill half the pitcher with either borage or plain ice cubes and add the garnish. Pour in the Pimms mixture until the pitcher is about a quarter full. Top with lemonade. Gently stir until combined. Immediately pour into a highball glass and serve.

Homemade Lemonade

This refreshing drink recipe is easy to prepare and at the same time impressive. The lemonade can either be served with Homemade Pimms and Borage Ice Cubes or straight up for children and anyone desiring an alcohol-free drink.

{ Makes 2 1/2 quarts }
2 cups tap water
2 cups superfine sugar
Juice and zest of 10 to 12 lemons
8 cups chilled sparkling mineral water

Bring the tap water to a boil in a saucepan. Add the sugar, reduce the heat, and simmer, stirring continuously until the sugar dissolves. Remove from the heat and set aside to cool, then refrigerate for at least 2 hours.

Prepare the lemons: Pour the lemon juice and zest and sugar syrup into a large pitcher and stir thoroughly. Add the mineral water. Serve in highball glasses over ice.

LEFT: Glasses full of refreshing Homemade Pimms.

Borage Ice Cubes

Borage is an annual herb with edible blue flowers. This traditional garnish for a glass of Pimms tastes like cucumber. The tender young leaves can also be added to a salad.

{ *Makes 10 ice cubes* }
1 1/2 cups still mineral water
10 borage flowers, washed

Fill an ice tray with water and drop 1 flower into each space. Freeze for at least 12 hours.

APPETIZER

My Mum's Lemon and Goat Cheese Soufflés

My mum used to make this soufflé as a main course along with a salad when I was growing up. Serve the soufflés in 4-inch ramekins as a starter for a wonderful taste of my childhood.

{ *Serves 10* }
2 bay leaves
1 onion, studded with about 10 whole cloves
4 whole black peppercorns
2 cups whole milk
2 teaspoons freshly grated nutmeg
3 pinches flaked sea salt
4 tablespoons (1/2 stick) salted butter
2/3 cup self-rising flour
4 large eggs, separated
2 teaspoons fresh thyme leaves
4 teaspoons Dijon mustard (preferably Grey Poupon)
Zest of 1 lemon
1 teaspoon cracked black pepper
1 1/2 cups crumbled goat cheese (from a log)

Preheat the oven to 350°F.

In a medium saucepan, combine the bay leaves, onion, and peppercorns. Add the milk, nutmeg, and a pinch of salt. Slowly bring to a boil over medium heat, then remove from the heat and strain into a bowl. Discard the onion, bay leaves, and peppercorns.

Clean the saucepan and return to low heat, then add the butter. Once the butter melts, add the flour and cook gently for a minute or so, stirring continuously until a smooth paste forms. Slowly add the infused milk, whisking to prevent lumps, and cook to thicken the béchamel mixture, 2 to 3 minutes. Take it off the heat and pour it into a large bowl. Add the egg yolks, thyme, mustard, lemon zest, a pinch of salt, and the pepper. Mix thoroughly, taste, and adjust the seasoning. Fold in three quarters of the crumbled goat cheese.

Place the egg whites in a clean bowl and add the remaining pinch of salt. Beat until soft peaks form. Gently fold the egg whites, 1 heaping tablespoon at a time, into the cheese and egg mixture. Do not stir vigorously or the mixture will deflate. Butter the inside of ten 4-inch ramekins and fill each with the mixture. Place them in a roasting pan filled with 1/2 inch of boiling water.

Place the roasting pan in the oven and bake for 15 minutes, or until the soufflés are set. Remove the pan from the oven. Let the soufflés reach room temperature.

Preheat the oven to 400°F. Sprinkle the remaining goat cheese on top of the soufflés. Bake for 20 to 25 minutes, until they have risen and are golden brown on top.

RIGHT: My Mum's Lemon and Goat Cheese Soufflés served with a watercress salad (see French salad dressing recipe on page 41).

family lunch

MAIN DISHES

Butterflied and Grilled Cornish Game Hens

This Leva family recipe is a staple. Michael and Marie often serve these delicious hens as they are easy to prepare for entertaining.

{ Serves 10 }
5 large Cornish game hens
1/2 cup extra virgin olive oil
1 tablespoon flaked sea salt
1 tablespoon cracked black pepper
1 cup whole sage leaves
1 cup fresh rosemary needles
1 cup fennel fronds

Rinse the hens. Cut the backbone from each hen and splay flat, breaking the breast bone. Drizzle with oil and season with the salt and pepper. Press the herbs and fennel fronds onto each side of the hens. You can do this prepwork up to 2 hours in advance and refrigerate until ready to grill.

Preheat the grill to high. When the temperature reaches 500°F, place the hens, cavity side down, on the grill. Immediately turn the temperature to medium and grill the hens until the skin is crisp and the flesh is fully cooked through, about 35 minutes. Rest the hens for 10 minutes before serving. If roasting in the oven, cook for about 35 minutes.

Spicy Peaches

Michael made me this dish during one of my first visits to his Connecticut home. The sweet and spicy peach combination is perfect with the Cornish hens or any grilled meat. The addition of lemon juice will prevent the peaches from discoloring.

{ Serves 10 }
10 large peaches
1/4 cup fresh lemon juice
3/4 teaspoon cayenne pepper
1 tablespoon coarse sea salt
1 tablespoon freshly ground black pepper

Submerge the peaches into boiling water for 10 seconds. When cool enough to touch, slip off the skins. Place the peaches on a serving plate and coat all sides with lemon juice. Sprinkle with the cayenne pepper, salt, and pepper. Serve at room temperature.

Layered Salad with Roasted Tomatoes and Lemon-and-Caper Dressing

We like to make this salad in a large glass bowl so you can see the gorgeous colored ingredients layered on top of one another. The lentils can be prepared a day in advance.

{ Serves 10 }
1 tablespoon extra virgin olive oil
1 onion, finely chopped
3 garlic cloves, crushed
3 cups Puy lentils
4 cups low-sodium chicken stock (preferably organic)
3 small bunches arugula

Layered Salad with Roasted Tomatoes and Lemon-and-Caper Dressing recipe continues pg. 87

LEFT: Butterflied and Grilled Cornish Game Hens on a vintage pewter platter.

family lunch

Layered Salad with Roasted Tomatoes and Lemon-and-Caper Dressing

2 ripe avocados, pitted and sliced lengthwise (reserve the pits)
3 small bunches watercress, trimmed
12 Roasted Tomatoes (recipe follows)
Lemon-and-Caper Dressing (recipe follows)

Heat the oil in a large saucepan over medium heat. Add the onion and garlic, and sauté until softened, about 5 minutes. Stir in the lentils. Add the chicken stock and bring to a boil. Turn the heat down, cover the saucepan, and simmer for 30 to 40 minutes, until the lentils are al dente but not too crunchy. Drain any excess liquid and set aside to cool.

Fill a bowl a quarter of the way with the prepared lentils. Layer with arugula. Next layer the avocado slices, along with their pits to prevent the avocado flesh from discoloring. Layer the watercress on top of the avocado slices. Cover with the roasted tomatoes faceup. Dress the salad with the Lemon-and-Caper Dressing and serve immediately.

Roasted Tomatoes

—

These tomatoes are also heavenly when served as a salad with fresh mozzarella and basil.

{ Makes 12 roasted tomatoes }
12 large beefsteak tomatoes
1 tablespoon flaked sea salt
1 tablespoon freshly ground black pepper
2 large garlic cloves, finely chopped
2 tablespoons extra virgin olive oil
1 handful fresh basil leaves, coated in extra virgin olive oil

Preheat the oven to 400°F.

Put the tomatoes in a large bowl and cover with boiling water. Leave for about 1 minute, until the tomato skins split. Drain the tomatoes and leave to cool. Peel off the skins.

Cut the tomatoes in half and lay upright on a baking sheet. Season with the salt and pepper and cover with the chopped garlic. Drizzle with oil and cover with basil leaves. Place in the oven and bake for 40 to 50 minutes, or until tender. Remove from the oven and cool before serving.

Lemon-and-Caper Dressing

—

This zesty dressing is perfect for summer salads. It will keep refrigerated for up to two weeks.

{ Makes 1/2 cup }
2 garlic cloves, finely chopped
2 teaspoons Dijon mustard (preferably Grey Poupon)
2 tablespoons fresh lemon juice
3 teaspoon tablespoons extra virgin olive oil
1/2 teaspoon sea salt
1/2 teaspoon freshly ground black pepper
1 tablespoon capers

Place all the ingredients in a glass jar and shake vigorously. If not using right away, cover and refrigerate until ready to serve.

PREVIOUS SPREAD. *From left to right, clockwise:* We toast to a wonderful family gathering. Spicy Peaches are the perfect accompaniment to Butterflied and Grilled Cornish Game Hens. Enjoying our mothers' company. LEFT: A clear glass bowl shows off the Layered Salad with Roasted Tomatoes and Lemon-and-Caper Dressing.

American-style Eton Mess

We added blueberries for an American twist on this classic English pudding. The pudding dates from the 1930s and was originally served at Eton's annual prize-giving, when parents and students picnic on the playing fields of this famous school. My husband (a Harrovian school graduate and Eton rival) felt strongly that we should name our twisted version the Harrow Mess. However, I demurred.

{ Serves 10 }
8 large egg whites
1 pinch kosher salt
2 1/2 cups superfine sugar
1 tablespoon cornstarch
2 teaspoons white vinegar
1 pint heavy cream
2 tablespoons powdered sugar
2 cups strawberries, hulled and cut in half
2 cups blueberries

Preheat the oven to 350°F. Line a baking sheet with lightly buttered waxed paper and set aside.

Carefully pour the egg whites into a large bowl and add the salt. Beat with a wire whisk or an electric beater until soft peaks form. Add the superfine sugar a spoonful at a time, beating until stiff peaks form. Fold in the cornstarch and vinegar. Spoon the egg-white mixture onto the baking sheet in the shape of an 8-inch circle, smoothing off the sides and top.

Reduce the oven temperature to 300°F. and immediately place the meringue in the oven. Bake for 1 3/4 hours. Turn off the oven and leave the meringue inside until the oven has completely cooled, about 2 hours. Do not worry if the meringue has cracked or crumbled as it will be broken up later. Set the meringue aside. It can be stored in an airtight container for up to a week.

In a large bowl, whip the heavy cream with the powdered sugar until thick and airy. In a large serving dish, break half the meringue into fairly large chunks and gently fold in the cream and two thirds of the strawberries and blueberries. Gently break the remaining meringue and place in the "mess," making sure to let some of the pieces poke out of the creamy mixture. Garnish with the remaining berries and serve immediately.

THE OUTCOME

As we sipped wine and revelled in juicy mouthfuls of piquant peaches and salty, succulent Cornish game hens, there was nothing else to do but toast the day. The evening chill prompted the end of the party as we packed Michael and Marie into the car to a chorus of fond farewells.

RIGHT: American-style Eton Mess neatly lined up on an old painted bench.

fancy dress party

COCKTAILS
Singapore Sling
Whiskey Sour
Sidecar
Lime Rickey

HORS D'OEUVRES
Blue Cheese Coins
Caviar Cream Puffs

Bagna Cauda
Chestnut Pâté
Wild Mushroom Beggar's Purses
Chinese Marbled Quail Eggs
Jonah Crab Claws with
  Curry Dipping Sauce

SERVES 10

LEFT: Crudités, with bowls of Bagna Cauda, are artfully arranged on bamboo trays.

A "fancy dress party" is the British term for a costume party. This type of event conjures up images of over-the-top dressing. There can be nothing more delightful than guests relaxing under the guise of another persona. Bruce and Wilson's mid-century modern Connecticut home is filled with rarefied, eclectic pieces from every decade of the twentieth century. The house and its vintage contents—a veritable history book of modernism—inspired the idea of hosting such a party. Michael and I happily colluded and concluded that this occasion should be a "decades" party, with each guest representing a fashion era from the twenties through the eighties.

THE LOOK

For a themed party, transform your space with decorative elements, tableware, and food that reflect the particular mood you want to achieve. Fortunate enough to have a backdrop already filled with Bruce and Wilson's antique collectibles, Michael and I found that very little effort was required to dress the stage for our buffet-style dinner. We served our drinks in twenties-style saucer glasses for champagne and used a selection of vintage martini glasses, highball glasses, and tumblers for the Sidecars, Whiskey Sours, Singapore Slings, and Lime Rickeys. Our food presentation evoked the saturated technicolor look of the fifties, a time of hope and prosperity. Once the tables were filled with food, we added decorative pieces, such as a bronze head and crystal tea-light holders, which reflected other eras.

Our guests wore vintage clothing from New York's Southpaw Design, which was in keeping with their chosen decade. I selected hard-edged eighties glamour in a Versace dress and a splash of red lipstick, while Michael in "Casino" fashion donned a sharp wide-legged seventies trouser suit. A sixties black-and-white dress, Vivienne Westwood bondage trousers, twenties bloomers, and a forties bias cut-silk number were among some of the other costumes gracing the room. The beauty of a decades costume party is that everyone can have fun reveling in the decadence of the past.

THE MOOD

Music

We bridged the gamut of music of each decade, from jazz and disco to rock and new wave, all played on premixed CDs.

Lighting

While soft lighting creates a relaxing atmosphere, make sure there is enough light to show off the buffet table. With this in mind we used a mixture of candles and low-level lighting. Interesting tea-light holders and candlesticks were placed next to dishes of food, and lamps were used for larger spaces and darkened corners.

Flowers

With so many beautiful objets d'art gracing the walls and tables, Michael and I chose a mass of simple white tulips so as not to distract the eye while at the same time providing a subtle perfume throughout the room.

Food presentation

A well-presented buffet adds polish to a party. Therefore much thought and consideration should be given to creating artful displays of food. Crudités look fabulous with an array of colorful vegetables. If you have the time, freshly cut vegetables are infinitely better than the precut store-bought variety. Michael and I opted for purple sprouting broccoli, zucchini, radishes, cauliflower, and bok choy, which we placed on simple bamboo platters.

Invitation

With a party that takes this much effort in both preparation and for the guests to assemble a costume, a written invitation is recommended.

THE PLAN

The day before

/ Compile to-do lists.
/ Go to the local grocery store and farmers' market to buy all the ingredients.
/ Prepare the Chestnut Pâté and refrigerate.
/ Bake the dough for the Blue Cheese Coins.
/ Make the filling for the Wild Mushroom Beggar's Purses.
/ Prepare the Chinese Marbled Quail Eggs.
/ Make the cream filling for the Caviar Cream Puffs.

The morning of

/ Set out vintage pieces on the tables.
/ Arrange the flower displays.
/ Make the Bagna Cauda.
/ Clean the vegetables for the crudités; arrange on a platter.
/ Assemble the Wild Mushroom Beggar's Purses.
/ Make the Curry Dipping Sauce for the Jonah Crab Claws.
/ Prepare the cocktail mixes and refrigerate.
/ Make the choux pastry for the Caviar Cream Puffs.

Last minute

/ Make the cocktails in large pitchers and chill in the refrigerator.
/ For the bar slice up limes, lemons, and oranges. Place maraschino cherries in small bowls.
/ Bake the Blue Cheese Coins and Wild Mushroom Beggar's Purses.
/ Assemble the Caviar Cream Puffs.
/ Assemble the platters beautifully and set out for all to enjoy.

CHEATS

The Jonah Crab Claws are a great cheat. We recommend buying prepared and prescored crab claws, which are widely available. This removes the dilemma of what to do with the leftover crab body. Rather than steaming whole chestnuts, buy a jar of steamed or pureed chestnuts.

Singapore Sling

Another cocktail from the early twentieth century, the Singapore Sling was created for Raffles Hotel in Singapore around 1910.

{ For each cocktail }
1/2 ounce fresh lime juice
4 ounces pineapple juice
Dash of angostura bitters
3/4 ounce Dom Benedictine liqueur
1/2 ounce cherry brandy
1/4 ounce Cointreau
1 1/2 ounces gin
1/3 ounce grenadine
1 maraschino cherry, for garnish
1 small pineapple wedge, for garnish

Fill a cocktail shaker with ice and pour in all the ingredients; shake vigorously for 30 seconds, then strain into a tumbler (or old-fashioned glass). Add the traditional garnishes—maraschino cherry and pineapple wedge—to each cocktail and serve immediately.

—

Whiskey Sour

Though this cocktail should really be called a Bourbon Sour, we think the sweetness of bourbon works better than a Scotch-blended whiskey. Depending on your preference, the drink can be made either way.

{ For each cocktail }
2 ounces bourbon
1 ounce fresh lemon juice
1 ounce Simple Syrup (recipe follows) or 5 teaspoons powdered sugar
1 maraschino cherry, for garnish
1 lemon slice, for garnish

Fill a cocktail shaker with ice and pour in all the ingredients; shake vigorously for 30 seconds. Strain into a small tumbler (or old-fashioned glass) and add the garnishes.

—

Simple Syrup

This key cocktail ingredient can be stored in a sealed bottle in the refrigerator for up to one week.

1 cup water
1 cup superfine sugar

Put the water and sugar in a heavy-bottomed saucepan and bring to a boil. Reduce the heat and simmer for 5 minutes, stirring until the sugar dissolves. Set aside to cool.

RIGHT: Classic Sidecars in elegant martini glasses.

Sidecar

Invented in Paris at Harry's Bar, this cocktail dating back to the First World War was the perfect vintage drink for our decades party.

{ For each cocktail }
1 1/2 ounces brandy
1/2 ounce Cointreau
1/2 ounce fresh lime juice

Fill a cocktail shaker with ice, add all the ingredients, cover, and shake until condensation appears on the outside of the shaker, about 30 seconds. Strain into a martini glass and serve immediately.

Lime Rickey

This is a refreshing nonalcoholic cocktail from the same family as the mojito. For those who wish for something with a little more bite, you can make a Gin Rickey by adding 2 ounces of gin per glass.

{ For each cocktail }
3/4 ounce lime juice
1 ounce Simple Syrup (see recipe on page 94) or 5 teaspoons powdered sugar
3 dashes angostura bitters
8 ounces club soda
1 lime wedge, for garnish

This cocktail is built in the glass as opposed to shaken to combine. To serve, fill a tall glass with ice and pour in all the ingredients and top with club soda. Gently stir with a bar spoon and garnish with a lime wedge.

HORS D'OEUVRES

Blue Cheese Coins

These cheese coins can be frozen in logs and defrosted when needed.

{ Makes about 80 coins }
2 cups all-purpose flour, plus extra for dusting
1 teaspoon kosher salt
1 teaspoon paprika
1/2 teaspoon cayenne pepper
1 cup (2 sticks) unsalted butter, chilled and cut into small pieces
1 cup crumbled Gorgonzola cheese
1/3 cup peperoncino jelly (or other sweet-spicy pepper jelly)

Combine the flour, salt, paprika, and cayenne pepper in a food processor fitted with a metal blade. Add the butter and pulse until the mixture resembles coarse meal. Add the cheese and continue to pulse until the dough starts to hold together.

Turn out the dough onto a lightly floured surface and knead quickly so the butter and cheese do not warm. Divide the dough into 4 equal pieces and roll into logs. Each log should be about 6 inches long and 1 1/4 inches in diameter. Tightly cover in plastic wrap and refrigerate until firm, at least 2 hours.

Blue Cheese Coins recipe continues on pg. 99

RIGHT: Blue Cheese Coins displayed on a Chinese lacquer tray.

fancy dress party

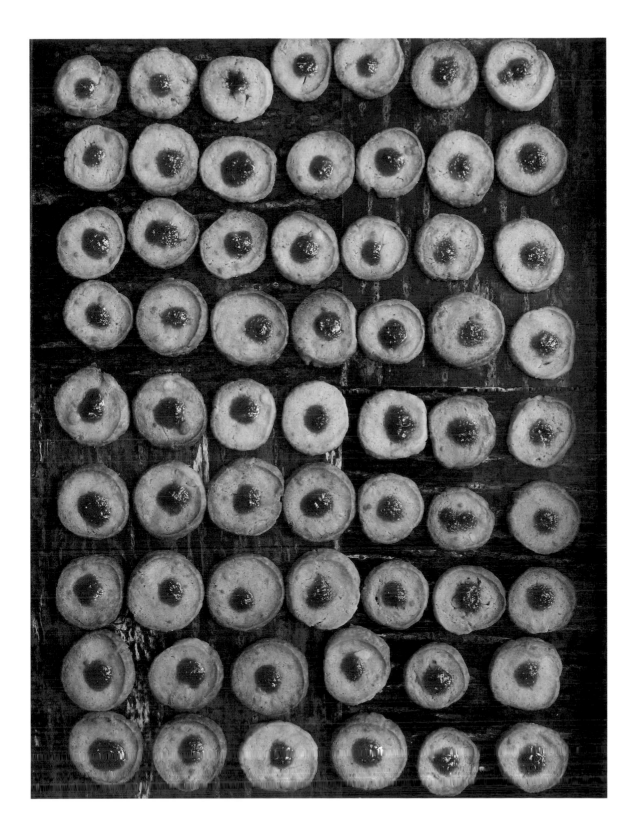

fancy dress party

**Blue
Cheese Coins**
continued

Preheat the oven to 350°F. Line a baking sheet with parchment paper.

Cut the dough into thin slices and place 2 inches apart on the baking sheet. Place in the oven and bake until lightly browned, about 20 minutes. Remove from the oven and transfer to a wire rack to cool. Spoon a small amount of jelly onto the center of each coin and serve immediately.

**Caviar
Cream Puffs**

Caviar Cream Puffs are the perfect plan-ahead party nibble as the choux pastry can be made in advance and kept frozen until ready to use. The choux pastry buns can also be filled with ice cream or whipped cream and drizzled with chocolate sauce to create profiteroles.

{ *Makes 20 cream puffs* }
1/2 cup (1 stick) unsalted butter
1 cup all-purpose flour, sifted
1 pinch fine sea salt
4 large eggs
1 cup heavy cream
1 cup crème fraîche
Assorted caviar (preferably a mix of osetra, beluga, and sevruga)

Preheat the oven to 450°F. Line a baking sheet with parchment paper.

To make the choux pastry, in a medium saucepan, bring 1 cup of water to a boil. Add the butter and stir until melted. Add the flour and salt while stirring vigorously until the dough forms a ball. Remove the pastry from the heat and cool slightly. Add the eggs one at a time, beating after each addition, until the mixture is smooth.

Drop heaping teaspoons of the mixture 3 inches apart on the prepared baking sheet. Bake the dough for 10 minutes, then reduce the heat to 325°F. Bake for an additional 15 minutes, or until golden brown. Remove the pastry from the oven and cool completely on a wire rack.

To make the caviar cream filling, in a large bowl, whip the heavy cream until stiff. Add the crème fraîche and stir until well blended.

Slice off the top third of each pastry puff, spoon in 1 teaspoon of the cream mixture, and top with a dollop of caviar. Replace the pastry lids at a slight angle and arrange on a serving platter.

LEFT: Caviar Cream Puffs look glamorous on a silvered glass dish.

Bagna Cauda

This dipping sauce is perfect served with a selection of seasonal farm-fresh vegetables cut for crudités.

{ *Makes about 2 cups* }
1 cup top-quality extra virgin olive oil
6 garlic cloves, minced
10 salt-packed anchovies, finely chopped
1/2 cup (1 stick) unsalted butter, cut into chunks

Pour the olive oil into a medium saucepan and add the garlic and anchovies. Place over low heat and cook 3 minutes. Add the butter, heat until melted, then remove from the heat. Whisk until blended, transfer to a serving bowl, and serve.

Chestnut Pâté

This festive vegetarian dip is surprisingly rich. I always serve it during the holidays when chestnuts are in abundance, with dipping vegetables or pita chips.

{ *Serves 10* }
4 tablespoons (1/2 stick) salted butter
2 celery stalks, finely chopped
1 onion, finely chopped
1 pound steamed whole or pureed chestnuts
1 cup fresh white breadcrumbs
2 teaspoons flaked sea salt
2 teaspoons cracked black pepper
2 cups organic vegetable stock
4 tablespoons brandy

In a medium skillet, melt the butter over medium heat. Add the celery and onion and sauté until softened, about 5 minutes. Remove from the heat and cool slightly.

Transfer the celery and onion mixture to a food processor and add the chestnuts, breadcrumbs, salt, and pepper. With the motor running, drizzle in enough vegetable stock through the hole in the top to give the mixture a soft consistency. Do not allow the pâté to become too dry or it will become thick and heavy. Transfer to a serving bowl and stir in the brandy. Cover and refrigerate until ready to serve. You can prepare the pâté a day ahead.

Wild Mushroom Beggar's Purses

For the filling use an assortment of wild mushrooms that are readily available. Encased in buttery pastry, they taste absolutely delicious.

{ *Makes 24 purses* }
2 tablespoons unsalted butter
1/4 cup olive oil
1 shallot, minced
1 1/2 pounds wild mushrooms, such as porcini, morels, girolle, and black trumpets, coarsely chopped
1 teaspoon fresh thyme leaves
1 teaspoon kosher salt
1 teaspoon freshly ground black pepper
1/4 cup white vermouth

Wild Mushroom Beggar's Purses recipe continues on pg. 102

RIGHT: Wild Mushroom Beggar's Purses for the taking.

Wild Mushroom Beggar's Purses
continued

8 sheets frozen phyllo dough, defrosted
1/2 cup (1 stick) salted butter, melted

In a sauté pan large enough to hold the mushrooms, melt the unsalted butter with the olive oil over medium heat. Add the shallot and sauté until softened, about 5 minutes. Turn the heat to medium-high and add the mushrooms, thyme, salt, and pepper. Cook for 5 minutes, until most of the water released by the mushrooms has evaporated. Deglaze the pan with the vermouth. Once the vermouth has been fully absorbed, remove from the heat and set aside to cool. Refrigerate if not using immediately. You can make the filling a day ahead.

Preheat the oven to 350°F. Line 2 baking sheets with parchment paper.

Place one sheet of phyllo on a work surface. Cover remaining dough with a damp dish towel to keep it from drying out. Brush the first phyllo sheet with salted butter and top with another sheet. Repeat until you have 4 layers. Cut the pastry into 12 squares. Place a teaspoon of mushroom filling in the center of each square. Scrunch the dough up from the center, enclosing the filling and forming a purse. Repeat the process with the remaining 4 sheets of phyllo. Place the purses on the prepared baking sheets, place in the oven, and bake for 15 minutes, or until golden brown. Remove from the oven and serve immediately.

Chinese Marbled Quail Eggs

—

These eggs are so pretty they will dress up any table.

{ Makes 24 eggs }
24 quail eggs
4 cups Lapsang Souchong tea, brewed extra strong
1/4 cup dark soy sauce
4 star anise
5 cloves
1 tablespoon flaked sea salt
1 tablespoon coarsely cracked Szechuan pepper

Place the eggs in a saucepan and add cold water to cover. Bring to a boil, reduce the heat, and simmer for 2 minutes. Gently transfer the eggs to a bowl filled with cold water and ice. Once cooled, remove the eggs and crack the shells gently all over, but do not peel.

Bring the tea to boil in a saucepan and add the soy sauce, star anise, and cloves. Add the eggs to the tea mixture and simmer for 2 minutes. Turn off the heat and steep for 1 hour. Remove the eggs from the mixture and peel them. Refrigerate until ready to serve. You can make the eggs up to a day in advance.

Combine the salt and pepper in a dipping bowl and serve alongside.

RIGHT: Chinese Marbled Quail Eggs set in a silver luster bowl.

fancy dress party

**Jonah Crab
Claws and Curry
Dipping Sauce**

This recipe takes so little time to make that I heartily recommend it for any time-pressed individual keen on throwing a cocktail party.

{ Serves 10 }
2 cups crème fraîche
1 cup mayonnaise
1 tablespoon minced shallot
1 1/2 teaspoons curry powder
2 teaspoons prepared horseradish
1 teaspoon fleur de sel
1 teaspoon cracked white pepper
20 cooked and scored Jonah crab claws

In a large bowl, mix the crème fraîche, mayonnaise, shallot, curry powder, and horseradish until thoroughly combined. Season with the fleur de sel and pepper. Then transfer to a serving bowl. Cover and refrigerate until ready to serve.

Place the seasoned crème fraîche in the center of a platter and arrange the crab claws around the bowl.

THE OUTCOME

Sipping Sidecars and Singapore Slings, our fanciful evening slipped past with each guest reveling in the role of a different decade. Chloe, dressed to the nines in her forties silk number, the epitome of decorum, watched bemused as a twenties flapper girl attempted a Charleston. Sophie, our sixties glamour girl "frugged" nearby. As our evening drew to a close, a full moon and clear night revealed the extraordinary sight of our costume-clad guests trailing down the drive.

LEFT: An attractive lacquer plate holds the Jonah Crab Claws.

new york brunch

DRINK
Homemade Ginger
and Lime Soda

MAIN DISHES
Goat Cheese and
Thyme Muffins
Roasted Cherry Tomatoes
Marmalade Breakfast Muffins

Herbed Polenta
Baked Eggs and Prosciutto
Marie's Asparagus, Radish,
and Scallion Toss

DESSERT
Sena's Lemon Zest Cupcakes
with Creamy Avocado Frosting

SERVES 12

LEFT: Our all-smiles little helper, Elio, gets the table ready for the brunch crowd.

I rarely brunch in England, saving that particular treat for my trips to New York City. When I observe the U.S. lifestyle, brunch is the meal that I most associate with this gregarious culture. After a hard workweek, Americans relish their weekends and enjoy the social pastime that a casual, impromptu brunch affords. I struggle to envisage a scenario back in England where I am able to get my friends to meet me before three o'clock. This makes breakfast entertaining impossible. Whereas when I'm stateside, I find the start of the weekend unimaginable without a hearty brunch. And so flirting with this American institution, on a Saturday morning we threw a Mediterranean-style brunch for our friends and their children in Pieter's airy loft.

THE LOOK

Certain formal brunches require a proper dress code, but a weekend brunch with friends, in our opinion, should be casual. To be dressy at such an hour is unnecessary; however, smartness shows a respect for guests and hosts alike. Our guests donned cashmere jumpers, blazers, and loose open shirts. Their outfits added a punchy splash of color around the brunch table. For a playful tabletop, we mixed Pieter's antique Italian paisley platters with simple drab ware and large lilac-gray napkins.

THE MOOD

Music Michael played a medley of Burt Bacharach tunes, which imparted a retro edge to the late morning. Whatever music you choose to play, it is important to keep it light-hearted enough for daytime listening.

Lighting With brunch being a daytime event, nothing more than daylight streaming in through the windows is necessary. At this gathering we were lucky enough to have Pieter's loft skylights and a beautiful sunny day.

Flowers For our brunch, we set out three 6-inch clear glass cubes lined with a banana leaf to hide the stems of a profusion of green-hued flowers on the table. Using a large green hydrangea as the central base to hold the other flowers in place, stems of mint, scented geranium, and hosta leaves were thread through. To fill out the arrangement, green celosia, lady's mantle, hellebores, and fuzzy green carnations were added. We particularly love these carnations as they feel chic and modern. The green color scheme worked beautifully with the table setting of amber glasses and vintage drab ware.

Invitation For a relaxed event like a brunch, an e-mail or a phone call is appropriate.

THE PLAN

The day
before

/ Compile to-do lists.
/ Shop for all ingredients.
/ Bake Sena's Lemon Zest Cupcakes and mix up the Creamy Avocado Frosting.
/ Make the Ginger Syrup for the Homemade Ginger and Lime Soda.
/ Juice the limes for the Homemade Ginger and Lime Soda.

The
morning of

/ Lay out serving pieces and glassware, and set the table.
/ Arrange the flowers.
/ Bake the Marmalade Breakfast Muffins.
/ Bake the Goat Cheese and Thyme Muffins.
/ Frost Sena's Lemon Zest Cupcakes.
/ Soak the skewers and skewer the herbs and tomatoes for the Roasted Cherry Tomatoes.
/ Blanch the asparagus for Marie's Asparagus, Radish, and Scallion Toss.
/ Line the muffin cups with prosciutto and fill them with the mushroom mix for the Baked Eggs and Prosciutto.

Last
minute

/ Prepare the Herbed Polenta.
/ Roast the tomatoes for the Roasted Cherry Tomatoes.
/ Finish preparing the Asparagus, Radish, and Scallion Toss.
/ Crack eggs into the prosciutto-filled muffin cups for the Baked Eggs and Prosciutto, then bake.
/ Mix up the Homemade Ginger and Lime Soda.

CHEATS

Brunch is tricky to prepare ahead of time, as guests arrive around eleven. As a cheat, the cupcakes and muffins may be purchased at a bakery. We have suggested that if you'd like homemade muffins, they should be made the morning of the brunch. Warm, freshly baked muffins are, of course, far superior to those baked the day before. Another cheat is to prepare them in advance and warm them in the oven once the guests arrive. A simple way to make the delicious homemade soda is to buy the ginger syrup from the grocery store, thus curtailing the workload in making the drink from scratch. There are also many natural sodas that make good substitutions for the homemade variety.

DRINK

Homemade Ginger and Lime Soda

This soda is a refreshing drink for adults as well as children.

{ Makes 1 1/2 quarts }
1/2 quart (2 cups) Ginger Syrup (recipe follows)
Juice of 12 limes (each freshly squeezed individually)
24 ice cubes
1 quart carbonated spring water, chilled

Pour the Ginger Syrup evenly into 12 highball glasses. Add to each glass the juice of 1 lime and 2 ice cubes. Top with carbonated spring water and serve immediately.

—

Ginger Syrup

If by some miracle you find that after your brunch you have some of the Ginger Syrup left over, it can be added to green or black tea as a zingy sweetener.

{ Makes 1 quart }
1 quart spring water
3 1/2 cups superfine sugar
3 cups roughly sliced, unpeeled ginger root

In a heavy-bottomed saucepan, combine the water, sugar, and ginger. Bring to a boil over medium high heat; lower the heat and simmer for 30 minutes. Skim the surface of the liquid, strain the liquid into a glass bowl, and set aside to cool. The syrup keeps in the refrigerator for up to 2 weeks.

MAIN DISHES

Goat Cheese and Thyme Muffins

There is nothing nicer than warm, fresh muffins for a special occasion. These goat cheese muffins spiked with thyme are perfect for those who like a savory taste.

{ Makes 12 muffins }
2 cups all-purpose flour
4 teaspoons superfine sugar
1 1/2 teaspoons baking powder
1/2 teaspoon baking soda
1/2 teaspoon fine sea salt
2 large eggs, beaten
1 cup buttermilk
4 tablespoons (1/2 stick) unsalted butter, melted and cooled
2 teaspoons Dijon mustard (preferably Grey Poupon)
1/3 cup finely chopped fresh thyme
1 cup crumbled feta cheese

Preheat the oven to 400°F. Line a 12-hole muffin tin with paper cups.

In a large bowl, mix together the flour, sugar, baking powder, baking soda, and salt.

In a separate glass bowl, combine the eggs, buttermilk, butter, mustard, and thyme. Stir into the flour mixture and gently fold in the cheese using a rubber spatula.

Spoon the batter into the paper muffin cups, place in the oven, and bake for 20 minutes, until risen and golden. Remove from the oven and serve warm.

LEFT: A vintage lattice tray full of Homemade Ginger and Lime Soda.

Roasted Cherry Tomatoes

As a Brit, I feel that the ritual of brunch would be incomplete without the English breakfast staple—the cooked tomato. This roasted cherry-tomato dish, with its intense flavor, is a definite improvement to the traditional British watery grilled beef tomato.

{ *Serves 12* }
24 long wooden skewers
60 large cherry tomatoes
1 bunch sage leaves
3 tablespoons olive oil

Preheat the oven to 350°F.

Soak the skewers in water for 30 minutes, as this will prevent the wood from burning in the oven.

Remove the skewers from the water. Thread a tomato followed by a sage leaf onto the skewers, alternating until each skewer is nearly full. Roll the skewers in oil and place on a baking sheet. Place in the oven and roast for 20 minutes, or until the tomatoes are tender. Serve immediately.

Marmalade Breakfast Muffins

Marmalade is a favorite British breakfast accompaniment. Having a proper title, marmalade has always been distinguished from ordinary jam. Spread it on a classic American muffin for a wonderfully zesty English flavor.

{ *Makes 12 muffins* }
2 cups all-purpose flour
2 teaspoons baking powder
1/4 teaspoon baking soda
1 teaspoon salt
1/2 teaspoon superfine sugar
1 tablespoon grated orange zest
2/3 cup fresh orange juice
1/2 cup (1 stick) plus 1 tablespoon unsalted butter, melted
2 large eggs, beaten
1/2 cup prepared marmalade with a finely shredded consistency
1/4 cup brown sugar
1/2 teaspoon freshly grated nutmeg

Preheat the oven to 350°F. Line a 12-hole muffin tin with paper cups.

In a large bowl, combine the flour, baking powder, baking soda, salt, superfine sugar, and zest.

In a separate bowl, thoroughly mix the orange juice, 1/2 cup of the butter, the eggs, and marmalade, and add to the dry ingredients. Divide up the mixture into the 12 paper muffin cups.

In a small bowl, mix the remaining 1 tablespoon melted butter with the brown sugar and nutmeg, and sprinkle on top of each muffin. Place in the oven and bake for 20 to 25 minutes until risen and golden. Remove from the oven and serve warm.

RIGHT: Marmalade Breakfast Muffins kept warm in a linen-napkin-lined bowl.

Herbed Polenta

The trick with this polenta is to stir like mad for the first minute to prevent lumps from forming, and then to leave well enough alone, resisting the temptation to poke and prod.

{ *Serves 12* }
1 tablespoon kosher salt
8 cups coarsely ground polenta
6 sage leaves, finely chopped
1 sprig rosemary
1 bay leaf
1 jar of prepared marinated green peppers
20 black peppercorns
1 cup (2 sticks) unsalted butter
2 cups finely grated Parmigiano-Reggiano cheese

Fill a large aluminum saucepan with 4 quarts of water, add the salt, and bring to a boil.

In a large bowl, combine the polenta, herbs, green peppers, and peppercorns. When the water has come to a boil, sprinkle in the polenta mixture, whisking continuously. After all the cornmeal has been added, continue to whisk for another minute. Turn the heat down to low and leave to cook for 30 minutes. When the polenta is nearly cooked to a thick consistency, melt the butter gently in a bain-marie. Remove the polenta from the heat and transfer the cooked polenta to a large bowl. Take care not to scrape the bottom of the pan. Pour the melted butter over the polenta. Sprinkle with cheese and serve immediately.

Baked Eggs and Prosciutto

A brunch with Michael is incomplete without his favorite breakfast dish of baked eggs with a slice of prosciutto.

{ *Makes 24 baked eggs* }
2 tablespoons salted butter
1/2 cup finely chopped shallots
1 1/2 pounds cremini mushrooms, roughly chopped
1 teaspoon kosher salt
1 teaspoon coarsely ground black pepper
1/4 cup crème fraîche
2 tablespoons finely chopped fresh tarragon
24 slices prosciutto
24 large eggs

Preheat the oven to 400°F.

Heat the butter in a large, heavy skillet over medium heat. Add the shallots and sauté until softened and lightly browned, about 7 minutes. Add the mushrooms and cook, stirring, until the mushrooms are tender and their liquid has evaporated, about 10 minutes. Remove from the heat and season with the salt and pepper. Stir in the crème fraîche and tarragon.

Lightly grease two 12-cup muffin tins and line each cup with a slice of prosciutto. The prosciutto slice should extend over the edges. Fill each of the cups halfway with the mushroom mixture, then crack an egg on top of each cup. Place in the oven and bake for 15 minutes, or until the egg whites are cooked and the yolks are still runny. Gently remove from the muffin tin and serve immediately.

LEFT: Herbed Polenta paired with an egg-shaped container of extra grated cheese.

Marie's Asparagus, Radish, and Scallion Toss

The secret to this salad is to blanch the asparagus so that it remains crisp. Make sure to discard any limp, overcooked spears.

{ Serves 12 }
3 pounds fresh asparagus
12 scallions, thinly sliced
12 radishes, thinly sliced
1/3 cup white wine vinegar
1/3 cup extra virgin olive oil
1 tablespoon finely chopped fresh thyme
1 tablespoon finely chopped fresh basil
1/2 teaspoon fine sea salt
1/2 teaspoon coarsely ground white pepper

Using a sharp knife, remove the tough ends and scales from the asparagus stalks and discard. Cut the spears diagonally into 1 1/2-inch pieces. Bring a saucepan of water to a boil, add the asparagus, then reduce the heat and simmer for about 6 minutes, until crisp-tender. Drain the asparagus and set aside to cool completely, then refrigerate for at least 1 hour or until ready to serve.

Put the scallions and radishes in a large salad bowl along with the chilled, blanched asparagus.

In a small jar, combine the vinegar, oil, herbs, salt, and pepper. Pour the dressing over the asparagus mixture and toss thoroughly before serving.

DESSERT

Sena's Lemon Zest Cupcakes

Michael's friend Sena invented these zesty cupcakes; they pair perfectly with her creamy avocado topping. They are just as delightful with a traditional frosting.

{ Makes 24 cupcakes }
Zest and juice of 2 lemons
2/3 cup canola oil
2 large eggs
2 1/4 cups superfine sugar
3 cups all-purpose flour
1 teaspoon baking soda
1 teaspoon kosher salt
1 teaspoon vanilla extract
1 teaspoon lemon extract
1/2 cup water
Creamy Avocado Frosting (recipe follows)

Preheat the oven to 350°F. Line two 12-hole muffin tins with paper cups.

Put the lemon zest and juice in a large bowl. Add the rest of the ingredients and beat with an electric mixer to produce a thin batter.

Sena's Lemon Zest Cupcakes recipe continues pg. 121

PREVIOUS SPREAD: *From left to right*: Brunch plated on vintage drab ware. A row of skewered Roasted Cherry Tomatoes atop a vintage platter. RIGHT: Marie's Asparagus, Radish, and Scallion Toss with ivory-handled salad servers.

Sena's Lemon Zest Cupcakes
continued

Spoon the batter into the muffin cups, filling them three quarters full. Place in the oven and bake for 20 to 25 minutes, until a toothpick inserted in the center comes out clean. Remove the cupcakes from the tins and cool on a rack for 15 minutes. Once the cupcakes have cooled completely, ice with the frosting.

—

Creamy Avocado Frosting

In Sena's light version of a cupcake topping, she replaces the butter used in traditional frostings with avocado. With lots of children attending our brunch, the avocado-frosted cupcakes were gobbled up in an instant.

{ *Makes enough frosting for 24 cupcakes* }
2 medium avocados, peeled, pitted, and roughly chopped
2 teaspoons fresh lemon juice
1/2 teaspoon lemon extract
1 pinch kosher salt
4 cups confectioners' sugar

Place the avocado flesh in a medium bowl and add the lemon juice, lemon extract, and salt. Using a handheld electric mixer, beat for 2 to 3 minutes, until the mixture is light and creamy. Add the sugar to the avocado 2 tablespoons at a time while beating the mixture. The frosting may be stored for up to 1 day refrigerated in a sealed plastic container.

THE OUTCOME

There comes a point when one notices that friends are beginning to nest and start a family. A brunch is an ideal way to entertain families because kids are naturally oriented to the morning meal. Pieter's penthouse apartment was a lovely setting for our brunch get-together. Smartly dressed children, surrounded by their parents and friends, were on their best behavior. With a nod to Michael's Italian-American heritage, we organized our brunch Italian-style, serving a deliciously buttery polenta (a Mediterranean alternative to the American South's grits) complemented by a crunchy asparagus salad. Food textures ranged from sharp juicy tomatoes to crisp prosciutto and runny eggs. We finished our feast with savory and sweet muffins and cupcakes, which were crowd-pleasers for the children and adults alike. Playing host and hostess, we watched bemused as our younger and older guests departed to enjoy the remainder of the day.

LEFT: Our cheerful assistant, Elio, and Sena's Lemon Zest Cupcakes on display.

private restaurant party

APPETIZERS
Spicy Squid Salad
Wild Mushrooms on
  Toasted Brioche

MAIN DISHES
Salmon Fish Cakes
Herbed Beef Tenderloin

Mashed Green Cauliflower
  and Celery Root

DESSERT
Dark Chocolate Mousse

SERVES 10

LEFT: Our waitress is suitably attired to match the occasion.

With a call from Michael and Matty saying they would be coming to London for a visit in the autumn, a plan to celebrate their overseas trip was born. We decided to throw a restaurant party for ten guests. It would require less effort than at home. All we faced was the task of picking the perfect space. We preferred the option of taking over a tiny restaurant but also considered back-room spaces devoted to private parties. Two Brydges, an exclusive London club tucked down a tiny alley barely a shoulder's-width wide, was the chosen spot. The restaurant, devoid of a sign, was only to be found by dint of two large pots of white hydrangeas flanking its narrow door. This Dickensian hidden gem with its air of cloistered comfort became our dining room.

THE LOOK

Part of the joy of a restaurant party is its ease. Select a venue that evokes the look and mood you want for your party. To personalize a party at a restaurant, create the floral arrangements yourself. The deep hues of the Two Brydges eggplant dining room dictated Michael's and my choice of flowers in shades of crimson, cerise, and brown to match the decor. The choice of attire ideally should echo the chosen establishment. Two Brydges, a perfect blend of British old-school members' club and the modern media set, is a cross between smart and casual. Following suit, boys wore open shirts and girls stylish dresses befitting a fall day.

THE MOOD

Lighting

The lighting in the restaurant is crucial to creating the perfect ambience for a particular occasion. Working with the restaurant's lighting, there was very little that Michael and I were required to do. However, we did bring additional glass-contained, unscented tea lights to set upon the long table. It is a good idea to have extra tea lights for a restaurant party, as an abundance of candles on a beautifully laid table is a welcoming sight. Always check with the venue about their fire code and other types of restrictions. Make sure to obtain approval for anything outside what has been offered.

Flowers

When selecting flowers, they should sit well with the decor of the venue. To fit in with the deep burgundy walls and heavy wood paneling of Two Brydges, we opted for burgundy and fuchsia dahlias, viburnum berries, and fuchsia, orange, and deep-red gerbera daisies, and we tempered the profusion of florals with leafy Cotinus coggygria (also called European smoketree). Black glass vases hid the stems of the flowers and also acted as a rich neutral background to the riotous autumnal colors. Create bouquets in your hand, then cut the stems the same length to fit the vessels. Once each arrangement has been placed in a vase, fill in the gaps with more blooms. Do not be tempted to overfuss; the arrangements should look natural.

| Invitation | Our restaurant party did not warrant anything more than e-mailed invites or phone calls, as it was a casual affair. However, we did choose to lay out place cards. Breaking a rule along the way would have delighted my etiquette-errant maternal grandmother, an English eccentric who enjoyed nothing more than to shock her peers. However, for a very special occasion like a prewedding party or holiday gathering, a written invitation is highly recommended. |

THE PLAN

A month before	/ Compile to-do lists. / Preferably a month or at least two weeks before the party, book the venue. Discuss with the manager the menu and other matters, such as flowers and special lighting. Ask if you are allowed to bring in your own flower arrangements and other decorative items. / Work with the restaurant to pick the wines to be served with the meal. / Visit the florist to see what kinds of flowers are available.
A week before	/ Go to the florist and select the flowers to fit the color scheme. / Buy tea lights or candles. / Contact the restaurant to lock in the number of guests. / Review the printed menu that the restaurant has provided.
The day before	/ Go to the florist and pick up the flowers. / Pack up the tea lights and candles and other decorative items to transport to the restaurant. If they have a storage space, drop off these items a few days earlier to avoid one less stress. / Make place cards or fill in store-bought ones. / Review the final printed menus that the restaurant has provided.
The morning of	/ Arrange the flowers in vases at home and transport to the restaurant. Alternatively, have your florist deliver arrangements.
Last minute	/ Lay out the flower arrangements, tea lights, and place cards. / Set bottles of red wine on the table(s) and make sure the white wine is placed in ice buckets. / Make sure both still and sparkling water are on hand.

CHEATS

There are very few time-saving tricks to throwing a restaurant party. However, should arranging flowers feel like a daunting task, order bouquets from a florist. Make sure the floral arrangements are delivered to the restaurant an hour prior to the start of the party. If you plan well, you will have time to pamper yourself before the event.

private restaurant party

Spicy Squid Salad

This is a fantastic recipe to replicate at home because it is so easy. However, the squid salad does require last-minute preparation, so bear this in mind if you would rather be spending time with your guests.

{ *Serves 10* }
1 1/2 pounds baby squid (calamari)
2 tablespoons extra virgin olive oil
3 bunches arugula
3 bunches watercress
1 cup roughly chopped fresh mint
1 cup roughly chopped scallions
4 oranges, peeled and cut into segments
3/4 teaspoon chile-infused extra virgin olive oil
1/3 tablespoon fresh lime juice
2 teaspoons runny honey
2 teaspoons fleur de sel
2 teaspoons freshly ground black pepper
10 lime wedges

Roughly chop the squid while heating the plain olive oil in a skillet over high heat. Add the squid and sauté for about 1 minute, stirring, until it turns white and opaque. Be careful not to over-cook the squid or it will become rubbery. Transfer to a plate lined with paper towels to absorb the excess oil and set aside.

Divide the arugula and watercress among 10 plates, making sure the leaves are mixed together and arranged in a central mound. Sprinkle the mint and scallions over the leaves. Place the orange segments on top.

In a small bowl, combine the chile-infused olive oil and lime juice. Add the honey and season the dressing with the fleur de sel and pepper, then mix through to combine the flavors. Evenly divide the warm squid among the plates and arrange over the salad. Drizzle with the salad dressing. Add a lime wedge to each plate and serve immediately.

Wild Mushrooms on Toasted Brioche

The combination of the buttery brioche with creamy wild mushrooms is divine.

{ *Serves 10* }
8 cups wild mushrooms (preferably a mixture of cremini, porcini, morels, girolles, and chanterelles)
4 tablespoons (1/2 stick) salted butter
1/2 cup sweet white wine
1 cup heavy cream
Flaked sea salt
Freshly ground black pepper
Ten 1-inch slices brioche
1/4 cup finely chopped Italian parsley

Preheat the oven to 400°F.
Wild Mushroom on Toasted Brioche recipe continues pg. 128

LEFT: Spicy Squid Salad in a crackle-glazed footed bowl.

Wild Mushrooms on Toasted Brioche continued

Slice mushrooms into approximately 1/2-inch-thick pieces. In a skillet, melt the butter over medium-low heat. Add the mushrooms, cover, and cook for 5 minutes, or until tender. Remove the cover, add the wine, raise the heat a little, and cook for 3 to 4 minutes, until the liquid has reduced by about a third. Pour in the cream and season with salt and pepper. Reduce the heat to low and cook through for another 5 minutes for the flavors to mingle.

While the mushrooms are cooking, place the brioche on baking sheets, transfer to the oven, and toast evenly on both sides for about 5 minutes. Spoon the mushroom mixture onto the toasted brioche and sprinkle with the parsley. Serve immediately.

MAIN DISHES

Salmon Fish Cakes

This dish is a great way to use up leftover boiled or mashed potatoes from the night before. Cutting out the potato preparation stage makes this a quick and easy supper. Serve with a good quality tartar sauce.

{ Serves 10 }
1 pound salmon fillet
1 pound potatoes, peeled and boiled
1/4 cup whole milk
4 tablespoons (1/2 stick) salted butter, melted, plus more for frying
2 tablespoons finely chopped curly-leaf parsley
2 tablespoons finely chopped sorrel
1/4 cup capers
2 teaspoons flaked sea salt
2 teaspoons freshly ground black pepper
1/2 cup all-purpose flour
3 large eggs, beaten
3 cups toasted white breadcrumbs
Light olive oil, for frying

Preheat the oven to 450°F.

Place the salmon on a baking sheet, transfer to the oven, and roast until cooked through, about 20 minutes. Remove from the oven and set aside to cool.

Meanwhile, mash the potatoes in a large bowl with the milk and butter until lump-free. Allow the potatoes to cool. Add the salmon to the potatoes. Fold in the parsley, sorrel, and capers. Season with the salt and pepper.

Sprinkle your hands and a plate with the flour to keep the mixture from sticking. Mold into 20 fish cakes. Brush the fish cakes with beaten egg and coat all sides in breadcrumbs. Freeze the fish cakes until ready to cook.

In a large skillet, heat 2 tablespoons oil over high heat and add 1 tablespoon butter. Fry the fish cakes in small batches on each side for 2 to 3 minutes, until golden brown. Since the fish cakes are delicate, use a spatula to carefully flip them over and to remove them from the skillet. After a couple of batches have been fried, refresh the oil in the pan, making sure to heat it first before adding more butter (at the same 2-to-1 ratio). Pat each fish cake dry with a paper towel. Transfer the fish cakes to a baking sheet, place in the oven, and bake for 10 minutes until cooked through. Remove from the oven and serve immediately.

RIGHT: Salmon Fish Cakes garnished with pea shoots and a dollop of tartar sauce.

Herbed Beef Tenderloin

As with any roast, tenderloin needs to rest after cooking so the juices that have bubbled up to the surface can be reabsorbed. While the meat sits, this is a perfect time to prepare the vegetables or other last-minute side dishes.

{ Serves 10 }
3 sprigs thyme, stems trimmed
6 sprigs rosemary, stems trimmed
10 sage leaves
1/2 cup (1 stick) unsalted butter, softened
2 teaspoons coarse sea salt
2 teaspoons freshly ground black pepper
3 pounds beef tenderloin, trimmed

Preheat the oven to 450°F.

Finely chop the thyme, 2 sprigs of rosemary, and the sage leaves.

In a small bowl, combine the herbs, butter, salt, and pepper. Rub the herbed butter over the tenderloin. Roll the tenderloin and secure by tying with butcher's string in 5 places. Insert the remaining 4 sprigs of rosemary under the string.

Place the tenderloin on a rack in a roasting pan, place in the oven, and bake for 35 minutes. Remove from the oven and tent with foil to retain the heat and moisture, then rest the meat for 20 minutes. Slice the tenderloin in thick pieces and serve immediately.

Mashed Green Cauliflower and Celery Root

This versatile side dish, with its fantastic chartreuse color, doubles as both a green and a carbohydrate.

{ Serves 10 }
2 celery roots, sliced into 1/2-inch pieces
Coarse sea salt
2 green cauliflower heads, woody stem removed and sliced into 1/2-inch pieces
2 cups half-and-half
1 cup (2 sticks) salted butter

In a medium saucepan, boil the celery root in salted water for 10 minutes. Add the cauliflower pieces to the saucepan and boil for another 10 minutes, or until the celery root and the cauliflower are tender. Remove from the heat and drain.

In a small saucepan, heat the half-and-half and butter over low heat until the butter has melted. Place the vegetables in a food processor and puree. Drizzle in the buttery liquid and pulse to combine. Transfer to a large saucepan and heat over medium-low heat. Serve immediately.

PREVIOUS SPREAD: *From left to right, clockwise:* A bounty of Wild Mushrooms on Toasted Brioche is one of the starters. The restaurant's intimate dining space and festive table make our guests feel right at home. LEFT: Roasted Herbed Beef Tenderloin and creamy mash are ideal comfort foods.

DESSERT

Dark Chocolate Mousse

One of my favorite puddings (desserts), this mousse can be made with just eggs and dark chocolate for those who are watching their figures. However, I do find that adding the cream makes for a lighter, irresistible texture.

{ *Serves 10* }
18 ounces dark chocolate, at least 70% cocoa (preferably Valrhona)
4 cups heavy cream
10 eggs, separated
1 cup superfine sugar

Break up the chocolate into large chunks and melt in a bain-marie or double boiler.

Meanwhile, in a large bowl, whip the heavy cream until soft peaks form. Set aside.

In a separate bowl, combine the egg yolks and sugar, remove the chocolate from the bain-marie, and add in the yolk and sugar mixture.

In a third bowl, beat the egg whites until stiff peaks form. Fold into the chocolate, 1 tablespoon of cream followed by 1 tablespoon of egg white, alternating between the two until all have been combined. Spoon the mousse mixture into 10 dessert bowls, cover with plastic wrap, and refrigerate for at least 1 hour to set before serving.

THE OUTCOME

Cosseted in our sequestered spot under the watchful eyes of an ancient portrait, we were a collection of friends, conspiratorial in our longing for celebration. Matty and Michael were our twin kings for the evening, holding court and titillating our English ears as our plates silently appeared, only to be removed just as quietly having been picked clean. The additional treat of throwing a soiree at a restaurant is the variety of dishes and being able to lean across to sample a neighbor's food. Fortunately, the dessert was the same for everyone. I am not sure how easily I would have forfeited a mouthful of my gloriously rich chocolate mousse. A restaurant party is a wonderful way to play the host with little to do but relax and allow the evening to wash over you.

RIGHT: A charming shaped glass for our decadent Dark Chocolate Mousse dessert.

afternoon tea party

SERVES 6

LEFT: A casually modern rendition of traditional British tea time.

An afternoon tea is a perfect occasion to catch up with friends. Though it is a highly cultivated English pastime with its own special etiquette, teatime can also be an informal affair. In place of a formal tea à table, Michael and I served high tea (an afternoon tea with assorted savories) to guests casually perched about Jordan's New York loft. The contrast of a classic high tea in a modern, minimalist setting was truly elegant. And so at the traditional time of four p.m., our guests gracefully grazed on delights, such as Extra-Lemony Drizzle Cake and Perfect Chicken Sandwiches.

THE LOOK

An American afternoon tea party is a female affair that evokes stylized images of fifties house-wives in flouncy dresses with nipped-in waists. There was nothing traditional about our tea party held at a Manhattan loft. This modern, urban twist was reflected in our guests' outfits of casual jeans and silky tops. Being British and having a penchant for dressing up, I was the only one wearing a dress, though I refrained from going so far as being hatted and gloved. Clad in slim-fitting jeans, Michael was the epitome of casual cool.

Michael's collection of Wedgwood basalt provided a contrast to the clean, minimalist white loft. To offset the black and white, we added a hint of color with purple napkins and a dark purple tulip arrangement.

THE MOOD

Music
The choice of background music can be anything that you fancy, be it a mix of your favorite bands or something a little more classical. However, we would draw the line at dance music, as it is inappropriate at a daytime event.

Lighting
Natural light should be sufficient; adding candles would be unnecessarily fussy.

Flowers
Arrange purple tulips in a few tall, clear glass pillar vases. Twist the tuberous stems of these blooms over the top of the vase at a forty-five degree angle and insert in the vessel. Then fill the vases with enough water to cover the flower stems.

Invitation
We love the formality of a written invite. However, the decision of whether to send one or not rests entirely on how casual you wish the event to be perceived. Should you plan on an afternoon tea party becoming a regular event among close friends, then forgo the invitation.

RIGHT: A study in black: Green Tea Madeleines on basalt and matching dark calla lilies.

afternoon tea party

THE PLAN

Three days ahead	/ Prepare the gravlax for Marie's Salmon Gravlax.
The day before	/ Compile to-do lists.
	/ Shop for all ingredients.
	/ Bake the Extra-Lemony Drizzle Cake.
	/ Bake the Green Tea Madeleines.
	/ Make the Lemon-flavored Butter.
	/ Hard-boil the eggs for Mrs. Matthew's Egg Salad Finger Sandwiches.
	/ Make the Court Bouillon for the Perfect Chicken Sandwiches and poach the chicken.
	/ Mix the batter for the Buckwheat Blinis.
The morning of	/ Bake the Fruit and Spice Scones if you do not wish to make them at the last minute.
	/ Lay out serving pieces and glassware, and set the table.
	/ Arrange the tulips as described in the flowers section on page 138.
	/ Prepare the cucumbers for the Quintessential Cucumber Sandwiches and place under a damp cloth on a plate.
	/ Prepare the egg filling for Mrs. Matthew's Egg Salad Finger Sandwiches.
	/ Make the Winter Berry Salad.
	/ Take the Buckwheat Blini batter out of the refrigerator.
Last minute	/ Slice the radishes.
	/ Cut the crusts off the bread for the tea sandwiches.
	/ Assemble the tea sandwiches.
	/ Bake the Fruit and Spice Scones if you have not done so already.
	/ Make the Buckwheat Blinis and add the gravlax topping.
	/ Plate the food.
	/ Make the Perfect Pot of Tea immediately after the guests have arrived.

CHEATS

The first cheat to consider for the Winter Berry Salad is buying precut grapefruit, as sectioning grapefruit is a fiddly job. We especially like Del Monte's Slightly Sweetened Ruby Grapefruit because the juice is not too syrupy for the fruit salad. Should you wish to go one step further, buy hard-boiled eggs for Mrs. Matthew's Egg Salad Finger Sandwiches. Be aware that if you use prepared roasted cold chicken for the Perfect Chicken Sandwiches; it will not have quite the same subtle flavors as breasts poached in Court Bouillon. But this time-saving option does provide a still-delicious alternative. For those who are determined to avoid the kitchen, it is entirely possible to purchase the cakes, madeleines, and scones. Make sure to shop at a good bakery as opposed to opting for their mass-produced packaged cousins.

DRINK

Perfect Pot of Tea

Michael introduced me to teas from the Parisian tea specialist Mariage Frères. I have grown extremely fond of their brand of tea and particularly like French Blue Earl Grey and smoky Lapsang Souchong. For best results for the Perfect Pot of Tea, use a bottled still spring water or just run the tap for a minute to make sure it has not been sitting in the pipe.

{ *Serves 6* }
1 quart still spring water
1 tablespoon tea leaves (or 4 tea bags)
6 lemons, thinly sliced
Skim (or low-fat) milk

Fill a teakettle with water and heat it. When the water is hot but not quite boiling, fill a teapot a quarter of the way with the water and remove the lid. Swirl the hot water around the teapot to allow the china to warm. Discard the water from the teapot once the kettle comes to a boil. Add tea leaves to the warm, damp teapot. As soon as the water begins to boil, remove from the heat, as overheating will reduce the oxygen content of the water and affect the flavor. Immediately pour the boiled water into the teapot and put the lid back on. The length of brewing time is personal and depends on how strong you wish the tea to be. As I like a medium-strength cup of tea, I brew for 2 to 3 minutes depending on whether I am making black, green, or white tea. Bear in mind that tea bags take less time to brew than loose tea leaves.

Once brewed, keep the tea leaves or tea bags in the pot and refresh with boiled water as needed. A slice of lemon may be served with any type of tea, though milk should only be served with black teas. Never mix lemon and milk in the same cup, as the lemon will cause the milk to curdle. If serving a black tea with milk, the done-thing in England is to pour the milk into the bottom of the teacup first and then the tea. My mother affectionately refers to pouring the milk into the cup last as "gypsy tea."

RECIPES

Quintessential Cucumber Sandwiches

Though I normally opt for homemade bread, an afternoon tea party is the time I veer away from my usual ideals and choose a store-bought presliced variety. We used Pepperidge Farm white, whole wheat, and whole grain breads for all our tea sandwiches. For this recipe we soaked the cucumber slices in vinegar to create a refreshing version of the Quintessential Cucumber Sandwich. The soaking is important, as it draws out any bitter flavors. You can use salted water instead of vinegar if you like.

{ *Serves 6* }
1 large cucumber
1 cup white wine vinegar
4 slices soft white sandwich bread, such as Pepperidge Farm brand
1 tablespoon Lemon-flavored Butter, softened (recipe follows)

Slice the cucumber as thinly as possible. Discard the ends. Pour the vinegar into a medium glass bowl. Submerge the cucumber slices in the vinegar and soak for 30 minutes. Remove the slices out of the bowl and pat dry with a paper towel.

Trim the crusts from the bread and thinly spread each piece of bread with butter. To assemble the sandwiches, lay a single layer of cucumber slices on the buttered bread, top with another slice of buttered bread, or leave open-faced. Cut into triangles or rectangles.

Lemon-flavored Butter

—

Flavoring butter is an easy process, and the subtle taste of lemon is a great way to elevate the most humble of sandwiches. You can also experiment with stronger flavors, such as garlic and rosemary, which are perfect for smearing on meat before roasting.

{ *Makes 1/2 cup (1 stick) butter*}
1 lemon
1/2 cup (1 stick) lightly salted butter, softened

Thoroughly wash and dry the lemon. Finely grate the skin, making sure not to shave into the white pith.

In a bowl, mash the butter together with the grated lemon until thoroughly combined.

Spoon the lemon-butter mixture to form an even log down the center of a 6 by 8-inch piece of waxed paper. Fold the paper lengthwise around the rough-edged butter log and roll the log back and forth to create a smooth form. Refrigerate to solidify the butter. The butter will keep for 2 weeks.

Radish Tea Sandwiches

—

For these palate-cleansing sandwiches, we used heirloom watermelon radishes. They taste the same as a common radish but are more beautiful to look at—with their white skin hiding a pale pink and purple flesh.

1 bunch radishes (preferably heirloom watermelon variety)
4 slices soft sandwich bread, such as Pepperidge Farm brand
1 tablespoon Lemon-flavored Butter, softened (see recipe above)

Slice the radishes as thinly as possible, discarding the ends. Trim the crusts from the bread and thinly spread each piece with butter. To assemble the sandwiches, lay a single layer of radish slices on the buttered bread. Leave open-face to show off the radishes. Cut into triangles or rectangles.

RIGHT: Radish and Cucumber Tea Sandwiches in front of a tangle of purple tulips.

143

afternoon tea party

Mrs. Matthew's Egg Salad Finger Sandwiches

These delicious sandwiches balance the savory flavor of egg with the sweetness of the pickle.

{ Serves 6 }
6 large eggs
2 tablespoons mayonnaise
2 teaspoons sweet pickle relish
1 teaspoon fresh lemon juice
1 celery stalk, finely chopped
1/2 teaspoon fine sea salt
1/2 teaspoon freshly ground white pepper
8 slices soft white sandwich bread, such as Pepperidge Farm brand

Place the eggs in a pot and cover with cold water plus an extra inch of water. Bring to a gentle boil over medium-high heat. Turn off the heat, cover, and let sit for 7 minutes. When the eggs are cooked, transfer them to an ice-water bath. Once cooled, crack and peel the eggs.

Coarsely chop the 6 hard-boiled eggs, place in a bowl, and combine with the mayonnaise, relish, lemon juice, celery, salt, and pepper. Trim the crusts from the bread and spread each piece with a thick layer of chopped egg. To assemble the sandwiches, top with another slice of bread and cut into triangles or rectangles.

Perfect Chicken Sandwiches

This simple chicken sandwich is sublime. For a little texture and spice, add finely chopped celery or a dash of cayenne pepper.

{ Serves 6 }
1 whole skinless, boneless chicken breast, trimmed of fat and connective tissue
1 quart Court Bouillon (recipe follows)
1 bunch watercress (large stems removed), roughly chopped
2 tablespoons mayonnaise
1/2 teaspoon fine sea salt
1/2 teaspoon freshly ground black pepper
12 slices soft whole wheat sandwich bread, such as Pepperidge Farm brand
2 tablespoons Lemon-flavored Butter (see recipe on page 142), softened

Place the chicken in a deep sauté pan and cover with the Court Bouillon. Bring to a boil over high heat. Reduce the heat to medium-low, cover the pan, and simmer gently for 10 minutes. Remove the chicken from the heat and set aside to cool completely.

Roughly chop the chicken, place in a bowl, and combine with the watercress, mayonnaise, salt, and pepper.

Trim the crusts from the bread and thinly spread each piece with the butter. To assemble the sandwiches, spread a thick layer of the chicken mixture on the buttered bread. Top with a slice of buttered bread and cut in half diagonally.

PREVIOUS SPREAD: *From left to right, clockwise:* An assortment of delectables enjoyed by guests in a chic modern ambience. A plateful of Fruit and Spice Scones, a British classic. RIGHT: Egg salad and chicken sandwiches are served on a pastry stand.

afternoon tea party

afternoon tea party

Court Bouillon

This is a great delicate-flavored stock for poaching chicken and fish. It can be kept in the refrigerator for five days or frozen until ready to use.

{ *Makes 1 quart* }
1 quart water
1 cup white wine
2 bay leaves
1 carrot
1/2 onion
1 celery stalk
3 sprigs thyme
1/2 tablespoon coarse salt
1 tablespoon mixed peppercorns

Place all the ingredients in a saucepan. Cover with a lid and bring to a boil. Reduce the heat and simmer for 45 minutes, then strain through a sieve.

Buckwheat Blinis

These blinis are the perfect accompaniment to Marie's Salmon Gravlax, as they are not too heavy. The batter can be made a day ahead.

{ *Serves 6* }
3/4 cup buckwheat flour
3/4 cup all-purpose flour
1 teaspoon baking powder
1/4 teaspoon fine sea salt
1/2 teaspoon dried yeast
3/4 cup warmed milk
1 large egg, separated
1/2 cup (1 stick) unsalted butter, melted and cooled
1/2 tablespoon canola oil
1/2 cup whipped cream cheese
4 ounces Marie's Salmon Gravlax (see recipe on page 150)
1/2 tablespoon chopped fresh dill

Sift the flours, baking powder, and salt into a large bowl.

In a separate bowl, mix the yeast with the milk and add the egg yolk. Pour the liquid mixture into the dry ingredients and stir thoroughly to make a smooth batter. Pour the butter into the batter.

In a clean bowl, beat the egg white to form stiff peaks and gently fold into the mixture.
Heat the oil in a heavy-bottomed pan over medium heat. Drop in tablespoons of batter; once the surface starts to bubble, the blini can be flipped over. Cook until lightly browned on the other side, then transfer to a baking tray in a single layer to cool to room temperature.

Smear the surface of each blini with a teaspoon of cream cheese and top with a sliver of gravlax and a sprinkle of dill.

LEFT: Marie's Salmon Gravlax and Buckwheat Blinis go well with champagne.

Marie's Salmon Gravlax

We love the subtle flavoring of Marie's, Michael's mother, gravlax. You must use the freshest salmon available, since it is not going to be heated through. The marinade will cook the flesh of the fish.

{ *Serves 6 (with leftovers)* }
3 pounds salmon fillet, with skin on
2 bunches dill, roughly chopped
1/4 cup sugar
1/4 cup kosher salt
2 tablespoons crushed pepper
Zest of 2 lemons
Zest of 1 large orange
1/2 cup vodka

Find a pan big enough to hold the salmon and line it with plastic wrap, allowing an extra 10 inches beyond all edges of the pan so that it can be wrapped securely around the fish once all the ingredients have been added. Scatter half the dill over the plastic wrap. Place the salmon skin side down on top of the dill.

In a bowl, mix together the sugar, salt, pepper, and zests. Rub into the flesh of the salmon and then sprinkle the remaining dill on the fish. Pour the vodka all over the fish. Tightly cover the entire fish with the plastic wrap. Weigh the fish down with a couple of cans of beans and refrigerate. Turn the salmon over every 12 hours for 3 days to allow the juices to cure both sides. After 3 days of curing, remove the salmon from the plastic wrap and marinate and wipe clean with a damp towel. Slice the cured salmon very thinly on the diagonal.

Fruit and Spice Scones

These scones are best when served fresh out of the oven. It is certainly easier to prepare them in advance, though; they can be popped in the oven for five minutes to warm through.

{ *Makes 12 scones* }
4 cups all-purpose flour
2 1/2 teaspoons baking powder
1 teaspoon fine sea salt
1 teaspoon ground allspice
4 tablespoons (1/2 stick) unsalted butter
1 1/4 cups superfine sugar
1 cup whole milk
1 cup golden raisins
1 cup dark raisins
1 large egg, beaten

Preheat the oven to 400°F. Grease a cookie sheet.

In a large bowl, sift together the flour, baking powder, salt, and allspice. Thoroughly rub the butter into the flour mixture with your fingers until the dough is a sandy texture.

In a separate bowl, whisk together the sugar and milk, then add to the flour and knead together, adding in the golden and dark raisins. Gently roll out the dough to a 1 inch thickness, and using a 2 1/2-inch round cutter, cut out the scones, taking care not to twist the cutter, as doing so will impede the rising of the dough. Brush the tops with the beaten egg, place on the greased cookie sheet, and bake for 15 minutes, until golden brown. Remove from the oven and serve hot.

Green Tea Madeleines

Madeleines remind me of Paris—each mouthful imbued with delicacy and refinement. In addition to serving them at a tea party, they are also marvelous to box up as gifts for friends.

{ Serves 6 }
3/4 cup (1 1/2 sticks) unsalted butter, plus 2 tablespoons, softened
3/4 cup all-purpose flour, plus more for the mold
1 teaspoon matcha green tea powder
4 large eggs
1/2 teaspoon fine sea salt
2/3 cup superfine sugar
2 tablespoons confectioners' sugar

Preheat the oven to 325°F.

In a small saucepan, heat the 3/4 cup butter until melted and lightly browned. Immediately strain through a paper towel into a bowl. Set aside to cool for 45 minutes.

Thoroughly grease a madeleine mold with the 2 tablespoons softened butter, then sprinkle with flour, tapping out the excess.

Sift the flour and green tea powder into a large bowl.

In a separate bowl, beat the eggs and salt with an electric mixer for about 4 minutes, until the eggs have tripled in volume and are thick. Gently fold in the flour mixture and the superfine sugar. Spoon the mixture into the molds, 1 tablespoon at a time, until each is three quarters full.

Place in the oven and bake for 12 to 15 minutes, or until the edges are a light golden brown. Remove from the oven, remove the madeleines from the mold, and cool on a cake rack. Dust with the confectioners' sugar and serve.

Extra-Lemony Drizzly Cake

This cake actually serves eight people. However, I prefer to slice six large pieces, as there is nothing worse than a meager portion of cake—especially this one.

{ Serves 6 }
1/2 cup (1 stick) unsalted butter, softened
1 1/2 cups superfine sugar
2 large eggs
1/4 cup whole milk
Zest of 1 large lemon
3/4 cup all-purpose flour
1 pinch kosher salt
2 teaspoons baking powder
3 tablespoons fresh lemon juice

Preheat the oven to 350°F. Line an 8-inch-round cake pan or a 9 by 5-inch loaf pan with parchment paper and grease with butter. Set aside.

In a food processor, beat the butter and 3/4 cup of the sugar until pale and creamy. Whisk in the eggs one at a time, then add the milk and three quarters of the lemon zest.

In a large bowl, sift together the flour, salt, and baking powder. Slowly add to the butter and egg mixture, 1 tablespoon at a time, mixing to combine. Spoon the cake mixture into the cake pan and bake for 30 to 40 minutes, until the cake is golden on top or a skewer inserted into the middle comes out clean. Invert the cake out of the pan and cool on a cake rack for 10 minutes.

Extra-Lemony Drizzly Cake recipe continues pg. 153

**Extra-Lemony
Drizzly Cake**
continued

Then transfer to a serving plate.

In a saucepan, mix together the lemon juice and the remaining 3/4 cup sugar. Place over low heat, then simmer until the sugar has melted and forms a syrup. Skewer about 20 evenly spaced holes into the top of the cake and pour in the lemon syrup until it has been completely absorbed. Top the cake with the remaining lemon zest.

—

**Winter Berry
Salad**

This fruit salad offers a light and refreshing alternative to the heavier dishes served at our tea party.

{ *Serves 6* }
2 large pink grapefruit
1 1/4 pints strawberries, hulled and sliced 1/3 inch thick
3/4 pint blueberries
3/4 pint blackberries
3/4 pint raspberries
3/4 pint red currants

Peel the grapefruit with a knife, removing the white pith as well as the peel. Supreme the segments by slicing between the membranes and releasing the flesh.

In a large bowl, mix the berries together. Add the grapefruit, squeezing the juice from the skin over the berries. Toss gently and serve.

THE OUTCOME

A tea party can be freed up from the rules that govern other forms of entertaining. In addition to serving tea, we offered champagne for those who wished for something a little stronger. By avoiding set courses, we allowed our guests to enjoy a playground of flavors that alternated between sweet and savory mouthfuls—sharp, sweet, sticky bites of the Extra-Lemony Drizzle Cake followed by silky Perfect Chicken Sandwiches. Without the confines of a table, our untethered guests were free to roam the room, nibbling on buttery Green Tea Madeleines and palate-cleansing crisp Quintessential Cucumber Sandwiches. Light conversation was washed over with hot cups of tea, warming us all the way through.

LEFT: The color of a vintage Venetian glass bowl accentuates the luscious hues of the Winter Berry Salad.

dusk
cocktail
party

Limoncello
Limoncello Martini
Michael's Negroni

HORS D'OEUVRES
Pappa al Pomodoro Shots
Tuscan Tuna Tartare
Spicy Salmon Ceviche

Tomato Herb Gelées
Pesto Torte
An Italian Antipasto Bar
Summer Tomato Bruschetta
   with Homemade Ricotta Cheese
Fava Bean Crostini
Sweet and Spicy Peppers Stuffed
   with Fresh Ricotta and Herbs

LEFT: Michael's gorgeous "growing table" is topped with an Italian Antipasto Bar and a Pesto Torte.

In a bid to hang on to summer for a little longer, Michael and I decided to throw a cocktail party in celebration of his heavenly garden. A Connecticut summer dusk is the perfect time for a cocktail hour, with its balmy temperature and none of the fierce daytime sunshine or gnats that turn even the best-prepared drink into a sticky mess. The desired effect is a throng of casually glamorous friends, milling about on a warm evening enjoying a glass of something as the sun sets. To counterbalance our lethal concoctions, we served a light mix of Mediterranean antipasti and Spicy Salmon Ceviche, presented on silver spoons.

THE LOOK

As much as we love to be casual, just once in a while it is fabulous to push the boat out by putting on a glorious cocktail dress. There is something wonderful about starting an evening in a demure outfit and watching the outdoor influence take hold as boys loosen ties and shirts and girls kick off heels to tread barefoot on the warm grass.

To create this feeling of relaxed splendor, we opted for unusual found items that glitter. In magpie fashion we used unconventional serving pieces made of mercury glass as well as vintage silver spoons on which to present our tartare and ceviche. The pièce de résistance was two silver balls filled with candles that hung from the pergola, much like updated disco balls, throwing out light over our silvery feast.

THE MOOD

Music

Music is very much a personal taste. It should be upbeat and loud enough to create a vibe, though not so loud as to overtake conversation or disturb your neighbors. We are fortunate enough to have a friend who is a DJ; however, there are also many good CD mixes that are perfect if you just have a sound system.

Lighting

The sun setting creates the ideal discreet lighting, while candles are perfect for after the light has gone down. We chose hurricane lamps and votives, which were set on tables and around the pool, reflecting beautifully in the water.

Flowers

With an abundance of lovely flowers and foliage in Michael's garden as our backdrop, we felt that to set out floral arrangements would be too much. Sometimes, such as this occasion, flowers simply are not necessary.

Invitation

This event deserves an inspired invitation sent in the mail. The invite itself should follow the theme of the party and be clean and modern, nothing fussy or flowery. We used silver ink printed on a handmade linen card for the ultimate finish. If you do not plan on spending quite so much money, here are some good alternatives. You can always make the card yourself on the computer, selecting a silvery gray tone if you have a color printer or plain black if you do not. We particularly like a sophisticated font like Baskerville.

Store-bought fill-in invitations should be simple with no images and a neutral color like gray or a pale blue; you can write in the details with a silver pen. For this party our invitation said:

Michael Leva and Nancy Parker invite you to a Connecticut Dusk Cocktail Party to celebrate the end of summer.
Saturday, September 20th, 6:00 p.m. until dawn
Michael's Address
RSVP to the above address by Saturday, September 12th, phone number

THE PLAN

The day before

/ Compile to-do lists.
/ Go to your local speciality food stores and farmers' market to buy all ingredients, except for the fish for the Tuscan Tuna Tartare and Spicy Salmon Ceviche, which you need to buy on the day of the party to ensure freshness.
/ The Pappa al Pomodoro Shots can be made the day before, though leave the final stage of adding the fresh basil and olive oil until serving.
/ Assemble the Tomato Herb Gelées.
/ Make the Homemade Ricotta Cheese.

The morning of

/ Prepare the Homemade Pesto, assemble the Pesto Torte, and toast the pine nuts.
/ For the Sweet and Spicy Peppers, combine herbs with the Homemade Ricotta and stuff the peppers.
/ Buy fresh fish for the Tuscan Tuna Tartare and Spicy Salmon Ceviche. Make the tartare and ceviche and refrigerate for at least 2 hours.
/ Set out the serving pieces and glassware for the bar.
/ Hang any decorations.
/ Make the fava bean mixture for the Fava Bean Crostini. Toast the bread but do not assemble.
/ Toast the bread for the Summer Tomato Bruschetta. Assemble at the last minute.

Last minute

/ Make cocktails in large pitchers, and chill in refrigerator.
/ Bring the Pappa al Pomodoro Shots to room temperature. Add the basil and oil and pour into shot glasses.
/ Heap the Tuscan Tuna Tartare and Spicy Salmon Ceviche onto mismatched silver spoons.
/ For the Italian Antipasto Bar, arrange the meats and cheeses on serving platters.
/ Top the Fava Bean Crostini with the fava beans and the Summer Tomato Bruschetta with ricotta and tomatoes.
/ Remove the Tomato Herb Gelées from the ice cube trays and arrange on a serving platter.

CHEATS

A cocktail party is a particularly easy occasion to pull off since you can stock up most of the antipasto bar items from your local speciality food store. Even a good supermarket will have all the required ingredients. The hors d'oeuvres are so easy to make they are almost cheats in themselves. To make the food preparation simpler, you can buy the ricotta (though our recipe is sublime), and even the tortes can be purchased. The trick is to make sure your ingredients are of the highest quality. But the most important thing to remember when it comes to throwing such a party is to have enough food. As most of the guests will not be eating dinner beforehand, you do not want them to either leave early with rumbling stomachs or, worse, to be intoxicated after an hour of enjoying the festivities.

Michael's mom, Maria, makes a huge amount of Limoncello every year. We use it for our Limoncello Martini. However, any liquor store will stock a commercial brand. Instead of spending money hiring staff, you and your friends' teenage children can make great waiters for the passed hors d'oeuvres. Reward them with a small present.

COCKTAILS

Limoncello

Michael's mother, Marie Leva, has been making this traditional Italian digestive for years for friends and family to enjoy. Limoncello can be stored in the freezer in an airtight container for up to three months.

{ *Makes approximately 64 ounces* }
11 lemons
34 ounces 160-proof vodka or grain alcohol
3 cups sugar
3 cups boiling water

Using a vegetable peeler, peel strips of zest from the lemons; reserve the lemons for another use. Put the zest and vodka in a glass bottle or other airtight container. Let stand at room temperature for at least 2 days, or up to a week.

Stir together sugar and boiling water until the sugar has dissolved. Allow the syrup to cool. Stir the syrup into the vodka mixture. Refrigerate in an airtight container overnight. Before serving, pour through a large sieve into a decanter. Discard the zest.

Limoncello Martini

This refreshing cocktail is a delightful Tuscan take on the classic vodka martini.

{ *For each cocktail* }
3 ounces vodka
1/4 ounce Limoncello (see recipe above)
Lemon twist, for garnish

Pour the vodka and Limoncello into a shaker full of ice and shake vigorously. Strain and serve in a chilled martini glass with a twist.

Michael's Negroni

The negroni is a favorite drink in Italy. I do not think I have ever been to a party with Michael without seeing him quaff one or two. Be warned—it is not a drink for the faint of heart.

{ *For each cocktail* }
2 ounces gin
3/4 ounce sweet vermouth
1/2 ounce Campari
1 blood orange slice, for garnish

Pour all of the liquors into a shaker full of ice. Shake vigorously, exactly 13 times. Don't ask! Serve in a chilled martini glass or on the rocks in a tumbler. Garnish with a slice of orange.

LEFT: An ideal accompaniment to an icy cold negroni is Sweet and Spicy Peppers Stuffed with Fresh Ricotta and Herbs.

HORS D'OEUVRES

Pappa al Pomodoro Shots

We like to serve this classic Tuscan soup in beautiful old shot glasses. It is a chic way to present this sweet and spicy hors d'oeuvre.

{ Makes 12 shots }
1 loaf stale Italian white bread
2 cups fresh ripe tomatoes, peeled and seeded (see Tomato Water recipe on page 164 for technique)
1/2 cup good-quality extra virgin olive oil
1 medium red onion, finely chopped
1 celery stalk, finely chopped
1 carrot, finely chopped
Fine sea salt
Freshly ground black pepper
Peperoncino
2 or 3 garlic cloves, minced
Handful fresh basil leaves, torn into small pieces

Slice the bread, removing the crusts, and soak in cold water for 2 minutes.

Pass the tomatoes through a food mill, or pulse to fine in the food processor.

Heat 1/4 cup of the oil in a sauté pan over medium-high heat. Add the onion, celery, and carrot and sauté until wilted, about 3 minutes. Season with salt, pepper, and peperoncino. Add the tomatoes, lower the heat, and cook for 15 minutes.

Squeeze the water from the bread and rub it between your hands to form fine grains. Add the breadcrumbs to the tomato mixture and stir in the garlic. Cook for an additional 15 minutes until cooked through, then turn off the heat. Add the basil and the remaining 1/4 cup oil. Cool to room temperature and serve in shot glasses.

Tuscan Tuna Tartare

We use mismatched vintage silver spoons to serve the easy-to-prepare, exquisitely delicious tartare and ceviche. They are sensual party bites, fun to spoon-feed yourself, or, if daring, others.

The delicate flavorings of the tartare dish require the best quality tuna and olive oil. The flowers of most herbs have a more delicate taste than the leaves. They make a lovely edible garnish.

{ Makes approximately 12 spoonfuls }
2 cups diced sashimi-quality tuna, trimmed of any dark spots or white nerve tissue
3 tablespoons extra virgin olive oil
2 teaspoons lemon juice
Zest of 1/2 lemon
1 tablespoon fresh mint, cut into chiffonade
1 tablespoon fresh basil, cut into chiffonade
Freshly cracked black pepper
Fleur de sel
Herb flowers, for garnish (preferably thyme and rosemary flowers)

Place the tuna in a medium nonreactive bowl.

Just before serving, add the oil, lemon juice and zest, and herbs, then season with pepper. Mound the tuna mixture onto spoons. Sprinkle lightly with a few crystals of fleur de sel and garnish with herb flowers. Serve immediately.

RIGHT: Tartar and ceviche on silver spoons sit in a bed of rock salt.

dusk cocktail party

Spicy Salmon Ceviche

The trick with this spicy ceviche is to add enough peperoncino to give a kick without overpowering the delicate fish flavor.

{ *Makes approximately 12 spoonfuls* }
2 cups diced sashimi-quality skinless salmon
1/4 cup fresh lime juice
Zest of 1/2 lime
1/4 teaspoon peperoncino
2 tablespoons extra virgin olive oil
1/2 teaspoon finely chopped chives
Fine sea salt
Freshly ground black pepper
Chive flowers, for garnish

Place the salmon in a medium nonreactive bowl. Add the lime juice and zest and peperoncino. Cover and refrigerate for about 2 hours, no longer, as the lime will "cook" the fish and cause it to toughen.

Remove from the refrigerator, pour off any excess liquid, and pat the fish dry. Put the fish back in the bowl and add the olive oil and chives. Season with salt and pepper. Mound the fish mixture onto spoons. Break apart the chive flowers and sprinkle on top. Serve immediately.

Tomato Herb Gelées

These gorgeous mouth-size gems look glorious presented on fresh leaves.

{ *Makes 12 ice cube-size gelées* }
1 3/4 cups Tomato Water (1 pound plum tomatoes)
1/4 cup dry white wine
Peperoncino
Kosher salt
Freshly ground white pepper
1 packet of gelatin, softened in 3 tablespoons water
Fresh herb leaves, for garnish (preferably nasturtium or sage leaves)
Nonstick spray

To make the Tomato Water, boil a kettle full of water and pour over the tomatoes. Let the tomatoes stand in the boiling water for 1 minute. Drain the water and set aside the tomatoes until they are cool enough to be handled. Using a sharp knife, pierce the loose skin of the tomatoes, taking care to avoid the flesh underneath, and peel back the skin. Once skinned, cut the tomatoes in half and gently squeeze over a bowl so that the seeds drip out. Discard the skin and seeds.

Puree the tomatoes in a food processor. Strain the tomato puree through a fine-mesh sieve into a small saucepan. The yield should be 1 cup of tomato liquid. Add the wine to the tomato water and heat over low heat until warm to the touch. Season with peperoncino, salt, and pepper. Remove from the heat and stir in the gelatin until it has fully dissolved.

Prepare a plastic ice cube tray by spraying lightly with nonstick spray. Pour the tomato mixture into the tray and chill until firm. Just before serving, run a sharp, clean knife around the edge of each gelée. Invert the ice cube tray onto a platter. The gelées should pop out. Top each gelée with a fresh sage leaf or an edible nasturtium leaf.

PREVIOUS SPREAD: *From left to right, clockwise:* Guests enjoying drinks and nibbles under updated disco balls. Grooving to laid-back beats as DJ Mattie spins the tracks. Enjoying a tipple by the pool, lit by hurricane lamps. RIGHT: A dish of gem-size Tomato Herb Gelées.

dusk cocktail party

Pesto Torte

This delicious, savory torte is heaven. Smear a large, indulgent scoop on crackers or toast.

{ Makes 24 servings}
1 cup unsalted butter, softened
1 cup mascarpone cheese, at room temperature
1/4 cup Homemade Pesto (recipe follows)
2 tablespoons toasted pine nuts

Combine the butter and mascarpone in a food processor and process until smooth.

Line a 7 1/2 x 3 3/4-inch loaf pan with plastic wrap. Take a third of the butter and mascarpone mixture and fill the bottom of the loaf pan with a 3/4-inch smooth layer. Top the cheese layer with a 1/4-inch layer of pesto. Set in the freezer until the pesto is firm, about 30 minutes. Top with a second layer of cheese and then with pesto. Set the loaf pan in the freezer again until the top layer of pesto is firm. Finish with a top layer of the butter and mascarpone mixture. Cover and refrigerate until ready to serve.

Remove the torte from the loaf pan. We set our torte on a cake stand covered with fresh grape leaves. Sprinkle the toasted pine nuts on top.

Homemade Pesto

Not only is this pesto divine, it is also incredibly simple and quick to make. This clever recipe can just as easily jazz up any pasta or rice dish for an instant wow. If you find you have made too much, just pop the extra in a resealable container and freeze. It will be good for a month.

{ Makes 1 cup }
1/2 cup basil leaves
3 tablespoons pine nuts
2 large garlic cloves, minced
3/4 cup extra virgin olive oil
1/4 cup finely grated Pecorino Romano

Blend together the basil, pine nuts, garlic, and oil in a food processor. Transfer to a bowl and slowly stir in the cheese.

An Italian Antipasto Bar

Here is our suggestion for different antipasti that work well together. We like to layer platters with meats and cheeses and reserve a separate dish for crudités. Use different flavored olive oils and salts for raw vegetable dipping. We broke the Parmesan cheese into pieces by digging a fork into it. Turn and lift up large, rough chunks. Serve in a bowl.

Italian salamis, such as Genoa or soppresata
Proscuitto di Parma or San Danielle
Gorgonzola or other rich Italian blue cheese
Parmesan, a reserve or aged Parmigiano-Reggiano, or Grana Padano

Other suggestions: A heady *bresaola* (air-dried beef) is a nice counterpoint to the sweet and salty ham. Fill bowls with mixed olives and the more unusual caper berry. Serve with Italian flatbreads, semolina toast, and breadsticks.

LEFT: A smorgasbord of Italian and French cheeses and caper berries served on a galvanized-steel tray.

Summer Tomato Bruschetta with Homemade Ricotta Cheese

A good time-saving trick for both bruschetta and crostini is to slice and toast the bread the day before. All you will have left to do is heap on the toppings at the last minute.

{ *Makes 24 brushetta* }
1 French baguette
1 whole garlic clove, peeled
2 cups Homemade Ricotta Cheese (recipe follows)
4 heirloom tomatoes (mix of yellow, pink, and red), thinly sliced
Coarse sea salt
Extra virgin olive oil
2 tablespoons fresh basil, cut into chiffonade

Preheat oven to 350°F.

Thinly slice the baguette on the diagonal. Place the slices on a baking sheet, place in the oven, and bake for 5 minutes, or until lightly toasted. Before serving, rub the surface of the bread with a raw garlic clove. Smear 2 teaspoons ricotta onto each toast. Top the brushetta with the tomato slices. Sprinkle with sea salt, drizzle with oil, and scatter with the basil. Serve immediately.

Homemade Ricotta Cheese

As this Italian cheese is a rather obscure recipe, when you make it you can indulge in fantasies of being a medieval-style domestic goddess. Don't let on to friends how easy it is to make.

{ *Makes 4 cups* }
8 cups whole milk
1 cup yogurt
1/2 cup fresh lemon juice
Kosher salt

In a large stainless-steel saucepan, bring the milk and yogurt to a simmer. Little bubbles will form around the edge of the pan and the surface of the milk will bulge slightly. Remove from the heat and pour in the lemon juice without stirring. Let it sit at room temperature for 1 hour to allow the milk to curdle.

Line a sieve or fine colander with 4 layers of cheesecloth, leaving enough hanging over the edges to gather up and secure at the top. Place the sieve in the sink and carefully pour the milk into the cheesecloth. Gather up the cheesecloth edges and secure with string or a rubber band. Tie the string to the kitchen faucet and allow the cheesecloth bundle to drip into the sink, or tie it to 2 wooden spoons and suspend over a large bowl for the same effect. Let the cheese drip for at least 6 hours or overnight. Transfer to a bowl and season with salt. Refrigerate until ready to use; it will keep for up to 1 week.

RIGHT: Summer Tomato Bruschetta with Homemade Ricotta Cheese and Fava Bean Crostini with vegetables from the local farm stand.

dusk cocktail party

Fava Bean Crostini

This fava bean mix can quite happily be made the day before and refrigerated until ready to serve, making it the perfect party antipasto.

{ *Makes 24 crostini* }
1 French baguette
2 cups fresh fava beans
1/2 cup imported Grana Padano or Parmigiano-Reggiano, broken into small bites
2 tablespoons finely chopped fresh mint
1 tablespoon finely chopped Italian parsley
3 tablespoons extra virgin olive oil
Coarse sea salt
Freshly ground black pepper

Preheat oven to 350°F.

Thinly slice the baguette on the diagonal into 24 slices. Place the slices on a baking sheet, place in the oven, and bake for 5 minutes, or until lightly toasted.

Lightly blanch the fava beans in boiling water for 1 minute, then plunge the beans into an ice-water bath. When cool enough to handle, drain and skin the beans and place in a bowl. Add the cheese, mint, parsley, and oil. Season well with salt and pepper. Just before serving, spoon a tablespoon of the mixture onto each baguette slice.

Sweet and Spicy Peppers Stuffed with Fresh Ricotta and Herbs

We love the striking, almost synthetic red of the peppers against the white ricotta. It is such a pretty hors d'oeuvre for a cocktail party.

{ *Serves 12* }
2 cups Homemade Ricotta Cheese (see recipe on page 168)
1 tablespoon chopped fresh basil
1 tablespoon chopped fresh oregano
1 tablespoon chopped fresh Italian parsley
2 tablespoons extra virgin olive oil
40 pickled cherry peppers, drained

In a large bowl, mix the ricotta with the herbs and oil. Stuff a teaspoon of the ricotta mixture into each pepper and serve.

THE OUTCOME

We began our evening as grown-ups, sedately listening to the birds, each other's murmurs, and cocktail music. An abundance of food fueled the party. Guests indulged their sensual side by spoon-feeding one another Tuscan Tuna Tartare and Spicy Salmon Ceviche. As the evening progressed, so did inhibitions regress. Mattie played DJ as we giddily danced with glee on the lawn, in the cornfield, and even in the pool, until the wee hours of the morning.

RIGHT: Michael and I enjoying one of his powerful negronis.

We awoke the next day from our midsummer night's dream of a garden cocktail party to heavy heads and an urge for comfort food. So with tousled hair, sleepy eyes, and a large flask of Bloody Marys, we headed to the local roadside diner to serve as our chef for our hangover brunch. We ordered hamburgers, onion rings, and milkshakes to soothe stomachs as we laughed long and hard over the antics shared at the dusk cocktail party.

Bloody Mary

A good Bloody Mary is the quintessential hair of the dog. A fine balance of savory tomato juice, warming Tabasco, and vodka will take the edge off. Celery salt and horseradish are the ingredients that round out the flavors and lift the cocktail from good to sublime.

{ *For each cocktail* }
2 ounces Grey Goose vodka
1/2 ounce fresh lemon juice
3/4 teaspoon Worcestershire sauce
1/2 teaspoon Tabasco sauce
1/3 teaspoon horseradish
4 ice cubes
4 ounces tomato juice
1/3 teaspoon celery salt
1/2 teaspoon freshly ground black pepper
2 celery sticks, for garnish
1 lemon slice, for garnish

Pour the vodka into a highball glass and stir in lemon juice, Worcestershire, Tabasco, and horseradish. Add the ice. Top with tomato juice and mix thoroughly to combine. Season with celery salt and pepper. Garnish with celery sticks and a lemon slice. Serve immediately.

LEFT: The ultimate hangover cure—Bloody Marys, burgers, and fries.

CONVERSION CHART

Liquid Conversions				Oven Temperatures			Weight Conversions			
U.S.	Metric	U.S.	Metric	°F	Gas	°C	U.S./U.K.	Metric		
1 tsp	5 ml	1 cup	240 ml	250	½	120	½ oz	14 g	7 oz	200 g
1 tbs	15 ml	1 cup + 2 tbs	275 ml	275	1	140	1 oz	28 g	8 oz	227 g
2 tbs	30 ml	1 ¼ cups	300 ml	300	2	150	1½ oz	43 g	9 oz	255 g
3 tbs	45 ml	1 ⅓ cups	325 ml	325	3	165	2 oz	57 g	10 oz	284 g
¼ cup	60 ml	1 ½ cups	350 ml	350	4	180	2½ oz	71 g	11 oz	312 g
⅓ cup	75 ml	1 ⅔ cups	375 ml	375	5	190	3 oz	85 g	12 oz	340 g
⅓ cup + 1 tbs	90 ml	1 ¾ cups	400 ml	400	6	200	3½ oz	100 g	13 oz	368 g
⅓ cup + 2 tbs	100 ml	1 ¾ cups + 2 tbs	450 ml	425	7	220	4 oz	113 g	14 oz	400 g
½ cup	120 ml	2 cups (1 pint)	475 ml	450	8	230	5 oz	142 g	15 oz	425 g
⅔ cup	150 ml	2 ½ cups	600 ml	475	9	240	6 oz	170 g	1 lb	454 g
¾ cup	180 ml	3 cups	720 ml	500	10	260				
¾ cup + 2 tbs	200 ml	4 cups (1 quart)	945 ml	550	Broil	290				
		(1,000 ml is 1 liter)								

INDEX

index

CREDITS

Prop and flower styling: Michael Leva

blissful beach picnic
Umbrellas courtesy of Confetti Bay

dusk cocktail party
Jewelry courtesy of 10,000 Things
Dresses courtesy of Philip Lim, pages 162
    and 163, and Peter Som page 163.
Men's clothes courtesy of Paul Smith,
    page 163, and Philip Lim, page 171.
Hair by Yuval Shemesh
Fashion styling by Nadia Ronchi
Planted table by Ken Selody, Atlock Farm

fancy dress party
Vintage gowns courtesy of Southpaw
Vintage suits courtesy of Cherry NYC
Makeup by Lottie Stannard
Hair by Gillian K

moroccan buffet
Carpets and pillows courtesy
    of Madeline Weinrib

private restaurant party
Fashion styling by Fiona Stewart
Location courtesy of Two Brydges, London

ACKNOWLEDGMENTS

When Michael and I embarked on this project, we did not realize quite the amount of work involved. However, we were fortunate enough to have a great team helping us, without whom this book could not have been made. First and foremost may we thank our publisher Charles Miers for believing in our project right from the start. Many thanks to our editor Sandy Gilbert—for all those late nights of scrutiny and for navigating us through the art of crafting a cookbook. To our brilliant art director Allison Williams and her team, J. P. Williams and Stacy Barnes of Design MW, we are eternally grateful for your endless good judgment and hard work. A huge thanks to our photographer Pieter Estersohn and his agents Jordan Shipenberg and Cheyenne Vesper at Art Department, who were incredibly professional and a true pleasure to work with. May we also offer a special thanks to Serena Bass for writing our lovely foreword. To Bruce Glickman and Wilson Henley for their generosity of spirit, wonderful house, and friendship. To Susan Matthews, a friend Michael has mentioned countless times, with a huge amount of respect and credit for being both a teacher and a mentor. To Michael's mother, Marie Leva, and my own, Gina Harris. Thank you both for encouraging our love of food and entertaining and for all the pearls of wisdom that you have given us over the years.

Finally, a heartfelt thanks to the many people who helped us tirelessly on our project:
Paula Bennett, Dave Bergman, Brigid Leary Blanco, Kathleen Boyes, Claire Cook, Amy Fine Collins, Ross Crookshank, Tom Curtin, Angel Dormer, Gaylinn Fast, Melode Ferguson, Libby and Terry Fitzgerald, Ricardo Halac, Henry Hargreaves, Stuart Harris, Tommy, Ricky, and Katie Hemelryk, Sonia Kashuk and Daniel Kaner, Shinsuke Kawahara, Anna Kirkwood, Richard Lambertson and John Truex, Jen Mallard, Maggie McCormick, Nick Michael, Jane Muss, Lucy Muss, Buck Parker, Pat and Philip Parker, Eric Pike, Anna Piscuskas, Marthe Reynolds, Ken Selody, Gay and Conrad Sheward, Lisa Smilor, Charlotte and Douglas Snyder, Neil Sperling, Susanna Sulk, Susan Swenson, Nico Evers Swindell, Sena Tang, Elizabeth Tighe, Vesna Trajkovic, Kim Truong, Susan Winberg and Ken Shewer, Linda Zelenko, and Janet Zheng.

First published in the United States of America in 2010
by Rizzoli International Publications, Inc.
300 Park Avenue South
New York, New York 10010
www.rizzoliusa.com

2010 2011 2012 2013 / 10 9 8 7 6 5 4 3 2 1

Printed in China
ISBN 13: 978-0-8478-3192-0
Library of Congress Control Number: 2009940391

Photography by: Pieter Estersohn
Project Editor: Sandra Gilbert
Book Design: Design MW